In the Best Interest of the Child

An Adoption Story

As told by
Mr. Hopeful

Chronicled by
Matthew R.S. Todd

Mill Lake Books

Published by Mill Lake Books
Chilliwack, B.C.
Canada
jamescoggins.wordpress.com/mill-lake-books

Printed by Lightning Source, distributed by Ingram

ISBN: 978-1-998787-10-4

This book is a combination of creative nonfiction and
fiction. Names, dates, places, events, and details have been
changed or altered for literary effect and to protect the
privacy of the people involved. The book is also part
memoir, and the conversations in the book all come from
the author's recollections and are not intended to be
word-for-word transcripts. Rather, the author has retold
them in a way that evokes the feeling and meaning of
what was said. Some events have been compressed, and
some narratives have been expanded. This is a book of
memory, and memory has its own story to tell. It is
recognized that others' memories of the events described
may be different from the author's.

Books by
Matthew Todd

Empowering Chinese Canadian Parents in Ethno-religious Communities Impacted by Generational Assimilation (Wipf & Stock Publishers, 2025).

What Does Athens Have to Do with Jerusalem? Eight Interdisciplinary Conversations Integrating Faith and Reason (Mill Lake Books, 2018).

Hope Alive: Going and Growing through Pain (Mill Lake Books, 2017).

The Crisis of English Ministries in Chinese Canadian Churches (Wipf & Stock Publishers 2015).

Historical Attitudes That Have Shaped the Church's Use of the Arts. (Word Alive Press 2010).

The Interface of Percussive Arts, Religious Experience and Sacred Association (Word Alive Press, 2008).

Dedication

This book had its beginning in the month of November (2019), designed in Canada as "Adoption Awareness" month. With this in mind, this volume is dedicated to those who have worked so ardently to assist in the process of an adoption, especially the many social workers who guided the Hopeful[1] family—the names are kept confidential in this book, but you know who you are.

Thank you to the Hopefuls' lawyers. Sincere gratitude is also expressed to the many family members who gave supportive comments during a long and difficult period of discernment. The Hopefuls thank their friends, their colleagues, and their life group, who gathered and listened to their adoption journey, encouraged them, and petitioned for them. Every time you just listened, it gave space to breathe in the midst of the heaviness that was being experienced.

Speranzosa

---

[1] Not their real name.

Preface

"Hope deferred makes the heart sick, but a desire fulfilled is a tree of life" (Proverbs 13:12 ESV).

Hope—being hopeful—is a virtue. It's the feeling of optimism you experience when you graduate. It's the anticipation you have about your future on your wedding day. It's that positive vibe you get when you land that career you wanted. And it's the joy and sense of assurance you have at the birth of a child, confident that something you want to happen will happen.

The story in this book took place in Cascadia. It recounts the complicated journey of one family, as told to me by Mr. Hopeful. It can be said that some parts of this story are fictional, but if you read it closely, like the fiction of C.S. Lewis, J.R.R. Tolkien, and George MacDonald, you'll find it tells true things. Like many of those stories, it will take you on a journey as things get difficult, get worse, and then get better, finally emerging into a new normal. People change, learn, grow, and mature, and people can heal by the grace of God. The story I am about to tell you is that of a couple and family I know well, as it was told to me.

This story finds its focus in a serious problem in the highest levels of Canadian social services. It highlights several ongoing unresolved difficulties:

1. Non-indigenous family members with mixed heritage children, who try to adopt those children, find they are being impeded and hindered to adopt members of their own families. This is done on the basis of "policies addressing colonialism" instead of seeking wholly "the best interest of the child."

2. An indeterminate number of partly indigenous children are having their right to be adopted by members of their biological families with a non-indigenous background obstructed by social services ministries. That denial is based on addressing historic government wrongs with colonialism and assimilation (politics) and not wholly on "the best interest of the child."

3. The issue of familial adoption of mixed heritage children should be looked at very closely because some bands' policies obstruct any adoption with true permanence and with true care; people related to the child should not be taken away from the child. There is a need for judicial oversight and accountability regarding how the highest levels of social services ministries assess placement for adoption of mixed heritage children. This is necessary to ensure that decisions are made to serve "the best interest of the child"—not to serve the political agendas of governments nor to produce statistical data that look favorable in the annual performance reviews of provincial agencies.

Table of Contents

1. The Family That Was 11

2. Losses and Breakdown 27

3. Recoveries and Transitions 31

4. Fostering: Safe Care... 35

5. Setbacks and Discrimination 37

6. Reflections on the First Summit 57

7. Reflections on the Second Summit 69

8. Reflections on the Supreme Court Hearing....73

9. Reflections on the Process 77

10. Adoption: A Forever Family 85

11. Saying Goodbye 89

12. Identity Formation:
The Long and Winding Road 95

Epilogue...103

References 105

Chapter 1
The Family That Was

As I reflect on our family's journey that led to the adoption of our biological grandchild, I can see much more clearly now the road we have been on. Messages in pop culture, the media, and movies seem to be mixed in how they portray adoption. Many of those depictions tend to lean towards comedy, such as *Annie*, *Elf*, *Teenage Mutant Ninja Turtles*, and *Kung Fu Panda*. Others, such as *Tarzan* and *Superman*, are a bit more fanciful.[2] Some film depictions of adoption are outright negative, including *Problem Child*, *Despicable Me*, and *Twins*. However, I have also been exposed to some positive depictions of adoption in the movies *Les Misérables* and *The Ten Commandments*.[3]

Adoption was also an academic subject that I had studied during my undergraduate years in my university's Psychology Department. But the subject was more than academic. In my larger family, I remember that my mother's sister was actually her adopted first cousin, who was half First Nations (her mother, my maternal grandmother's sister, died of tuberculosis). I took it for granted that she was my

---

[2] Tara McNamara, "The 15 Top Family Films About Adoption," *Huffpost*, December 6, 2017, accessed Dec. 13, 2019: https://www.huffpost.com/entry/the-top-15-family-films-a_b_6331544

[3] E. Young, "We can do better on depictions of adoption in pop culture," *Global Comment*, May 22, 2018, accessed December 13, 2019: http://globalcomment.com/we-can-do-better-on-depictions-of-adoption-in-pop-culture/

aunt and was never curious enough as a youth to ask questions. I knew I also had a second cousin who had been adopted by my paternal great aunt. I have another second cousin who shared with us some genealogical research about the paternal side of the family. Census data showed that in our ancestral line there were families in the 1800s and earlier in which grandchildren were being raised in their grandparents' homes. After I graduated from high school, my grandfather took me to a restaurant and told me that ten months after he returned from World War Two (in August 1946), he and my grandmother gave up a newborn child for adoption. I could hardly believe my ears. This had been a family secret, and I was not to repeat that I knew to my grandmother or it would upset her. So, I kept this to myself. Later, I was introduced to this aunt and uncle-in-law during my university undergraduate years. I never disclosed to my son that I had an adopted-out aunt and that I would visit with her and my uncle-in-law when they were on vacation from the university they worked at and traveled to our area. I was concerned that my son would slip and mention it to my grandmother while she was living, and I did not want to upset her. When my grandmother died, I told my son he had a great-aunt.

It was through my aunt's retelling of her adopted life experience that I gained a window into what it felt like to be adopted out. I was emotionally moved at the complications and the emotional freight of it all. When my grandmother died, I conducted the funeral, with the mayor of the city giving a speech. My grandfather had his daughter (my adopted-out aunt) stand in the family condolence lineup to shake the hands of friends, family members, dignitaries, and community members. My grandfather introduced her as his biological daughter (a fact). There was a lot of shock as my grandmother had been a politician for the city and her friendship circle included political and civic leaders. My grandfather had had a full career with the city. They were well known in the community and in the media. In their generation, adoptions were never spoken of in public.[4] My grandfather "came out of the closet," so to speak, at the age of ninety, declaring that he had a daughter with whom he had maintained a relationship for more than forty years and that he refused to keep secrets about it anymore. He told me that from the day she was adopted out, there wasn't a single day he didn't think about her. I am still deeply moved thinking about this.

Split Generation Families

Despite all of this, I still had little knowledge of the adoption process, why or how children were adopted, and the emotional and psychological dimensions of adoption. Engaging in the adoption of a grandchild helped me to reflect on the fact that my grandparents had an enormous influence in helping to raise me when I was young. I am now a grandparent myself, one of the 7.5 million grandparents aged 45 and older in Canada.[5] A growing number of grandparents in this

---

[4] A peer of my grandfather was the late Jack Wester, who similarly had a daughter in 1936 and gave her up for adoption — "the experience emotionally shattered his wife...[who] worked hard to trace the lost daughter." "Jack Wester (Obituary)," *The Canadian Encyclopedia*, Dec. 15, 2013, accessed July 5, 2021: https://www.thecanadianencyclopedia.ca/en/article/jack-webster-obituary

[5] The Vanier Institute of the Family, "National Grandparents Day: New insights from Canadian Research," September 8, 2022, accessed April 9, 2023: https://vanierinstitute.ca/national-

country are living with and caring for their grandchildren—and, for many, it is not easy. Statistics Canada noted that in 2011 close to 600,000 grandparents aged 45 and older, or about 8% of all grandparents in this age group in Canada, lived in the same household as their grandchildren; 12% of these grandparents were in "skipped generation" households, that is, with no middle generation present. Looking at this issue from the opposite direction, of the 8.9 million children aged 24 and under who lived in a census family in 2011, more than 650,000, or 7%, co-resided with their grandparents; 9% of these lived solely with their grandparents.[6]

It has been noted that only recently has the topic of grandparents raising grandchildren begun to receive attention from the media, politicians, and researchers. Hayslip and Kaminski have cited American statistics showing that "custodial grandparents...caring for their grandchildren on a full-time basis [is] becoming more prevalent."[7] The estimation is that over "2.4 million individuals [are]

---

grandparents-day-new-insights-from-canadian-research/#:~:text=Regardless%20of%20where%20they%20live,a%20happy%20National%20Grandparents'%20Day!

[6] Statistics Canada, "Grandparents living with their grandchildren, 2011," May 14, 2015, accessed June 21, 2023: https://www150.statcan.gc.ca/n1/daily-quotidien/150414/dq150414a-eng.htm. Also see: Statistics Canada, "Diversity of grandparents living with their grandchildren," April 14, 2015, accessed June 21, 2023: https://www150.statcan.gc.ca/n1/pub/75-006-x/2015001/article/14154-eng.pdf

[7] Bert Hayslip and Patricia L. Kaminski, "Grandparents Raising their Grandchildren: A Review of the Literature and Suggestions for Practice," *The Gerontologist*, Vol. 45, No. 2 (2005), 262.

raising their grandchildren [and that] since 1990, there has been a 30% increase in the number of children...living in households maintained by grandparents."[8] Statistics Canada (2003) data indicate that between 1991 and 2001 there was a 20% increase in the number of Canadian children under 18 who were living with grandparents with no parent present in the home; there were almost 27,000 Canadian grandparents raising grandchildren in skipped generation families in 1996.[9]

Fuller-Thomas indicates that "it is still rare for grandparents to take over sole caregiving responsibility as is the case in skipped generation households in which they perform all the functions that were traditionally provided by the parent." Milan and Hamm reported that in 2001 there were 56,700 Canadian grandparents in skipped generation households.[10] A more recent 2015 figure is that "more than one in ten [are] the sole caregivers of their grandchildren...[some] call it the club that none of us wanted to join [where] our 'freedom 55' plan is now the 'work until we die' plan."[11] Statements such as that

---

[8] Ibid.

[9] Esme Fuller-Thomson, "Grandparents Raising Grandchildren in Canada: A Profile of Skipped Generation Families" (Working paper No. 132), Hamilton, Ontario: SEDAP, McMaster University, 2005, 2.

[10] Anne Milan and Brian Hamm, "Across the generations: Grandparents and grandchildren." *Canadian Social Trends*, Winter 2003, accessed April 8, 2023: https://www.150.statcan.gc.ca/n1/en/pub/11-008-x/2003003/article/6619-eng.pdf?st=0AOcjSku

[11] City News, "Many Canadians are raising their grandchildren: Statistics Canada," Vancouver News 1130, April 14, 2015, accessed April 9, 2023:

underline how difficult making a decision to be the primary caregiver to a grandchild can be.

New Family Life

The story in our own immediate family involves our son Jack.[12] My wife and I were married almost ten years before we had our son. He was a planned and wanted child. He was born when I was thirty-one. I had finished university, and I owned everything in my home—except that I needed to complete paying off a mortgage. I remember the day he was born. The hospital called the company I was working for to release me to be with my wife at the birth of our child. However, the company had two men with the same last name (those were the days before universal cell phone ownership). I was working in one city, and the other employee was working in another city. The supervisor drove to the other city to tell the other employee, who was older, that his wife was having a baby; the supervisor said he would take over the food sales route and allow the other man to drive the supervisor's car to the hospital. When the supervisor told the other salesman his wife was having a baby, he replied, "She'd better not be having a baby!" Realizing that he had made a mistake, the supervisor came looking for me. Because our extended family had waited ten years for us to get through university and college and in established jobs, our son was warmly welcomed by the whole family and would be somewhat spoiled as an only child. He was raised in a good home with both biological parents in a middle-

---

https://vancouver.citynews.ca/2015/04/14/many-canadians-are-raising-their-grandchildren-statistics-canada/

[12] Again, not his real name.

class, hardworking family. Our marriage is a good marriage, and our son benefited from having two working parents and having all his needs taken care of to the best of our abilities. I put him in every sport I could enroll him in—soccer, baseball, lacrosse, floor hockey, and swimming. For years, we had him in private piano lessons, and he also tried trumpet and clarinet one year. We raised him in a caring community, and he was enrolled in youth programs and summer camps. He did not lack for anything, being in a home with two hard-working parents who loved him and who were focused on his well-being.

Our early family planning was to have two children, but my wife experienced a serious injury the year we were planning to expand our family and undertake construction of a new home. My wife's healing took three years. Because of this, we did not have another child, nor did we continue with the building project. Fourteen years later, we became empty nesters. When our household was quiet and empty, I reflected on the fact that we had really desired to have two children and missed the chance because our bodies and circumstances had transitioned us into a different stage of life. I suppose there are many reasons I could offer as to why having two children—preferably not twenty-two years apart—might be a good idea. But one thing stands out in my mind. We don't have children only when they are minors. We have children for our whole lives. Family is not a short-term proposition. If we can see past the burden of raising children, we will realize that the relationships can endure through all the seasons of our lives.

Challenges

By the time our son Jack was in about grade three, we slowly realized he was very challenged behaviorally. We consulted his teacher, the school counselor, a youth worker, our family doctor, and a pediatrician. Further assessment was done through the children's hospital, and the conclusion was that he had attention-deficit/hyperactivity disorder (ADHD), as well as some neurological clinical issues. This helped us as parents come to terms with some of his mental health challenges and empowered us to advocate for him in the school system and community. All of this was very challenging. We offered to participate in his classroom field trips. I even taught a grade two class on music and brought in my musical instruments—Jack gained rock star status for a day with his father coming in to teach the music class. I tried everything I could to keep him active in extracurricular activities such as swimming, skating, and regular weekly attendance at a youth group.

Apart from some of these mental health challenges, my wife and I attempted to carry on family life in normal ways. We had a family night every Friday where we would watch a movie together with snacks, we had annual vacations together (camping on one of the Gulf Islands, a trip to Disneyland one year, a trip to the Grand Canyon, road trips to Whistler and Seattle, and so forth). We maintained a middle-class family life in a home that we owned, and we worked hard at sustaining a balanced lifestyle. We worked hard at communicating to our son that he was loved by us, his family, and God and that he was willed into existence for a purpose.

My wife and I had both embraced the worldviews of our families in our youth, and we were actively involved in a warm community (especially musically) throughout all the years Jack was growing up in our home. Jack was raised with grace-based role models—not perfect people by any means—but parents who embraced the mystery of life and endeavored to revel in the goodness of being. We desired to live this out in practical ways. When Jack was between the ages of seven and nineteen, I was also actively serving in my community. This provided some perks for Jack, as many participants in the community were good to him in providing gifts (especially during Christmas). Our son remembers their kindness fondly. I often orchestrated opportunities for my son to interact with other children and teen youth workers.

One of the things that parents of a child with ADHD experience is the frequent, unpredictable calls that they receive from the school to address the youth's behavior. The behavior could include inattention in class, forgetting homework, difficulty organizing tasks, inability to foresee the consequences of actions, inability to perceive social clues that indicate his behavior is unacceptable, and impulsiveness. It can be exhausting. I used to look forward to summer holidays just to get a break from all the pressure this created. We attended many types of training and workshops on topics such as "attachment theory," and "youth work," so that we could navigate the challenges we experienced with our son and try to support him with the struggles that he experienced while in the public school system. He was getting by in the public school system, but it wasn't great as he struggled with structure and struggled to keep focused on academics. And then, when he was sixteen, the unimaginable happened.

New Trauma

One Thanksgiving Day, our extended family had planned a dinner for 6:00 p.m. We received a phone call telling us that Jack was in the hospital and we needed to get there quickly. We weren't told what had happened. We arrived at the hospital to find an RCMP officer present and our son waiting for surgery to remove metal from his bleeding neck. We were completely shocked to find out what had led up to this situation.

Apparently, Jack had been randomly and violently assaulted. He had been waiting at the bus stop across the street from our home. While neighbors were cutting their lawns and playing with their kids outside, a carload of three older teens came slowly cruising through the area. Jack later told us that he didn't like the way that they were looking at him while he was standing at the bus stop. He felt intimidated. Then the car turned around and accelerated towards our son. The occupants rolled down the windows of the car, pulled out two Walther P99 replica pellet guns, and began firing shots (steel pellets, the kind that are often used to kill birds or squirrels) into Jack's body. One of the pellets penetrated his neck. He realized he had been hit when he placed his hand on his neck and the hand became covered in blood.

As the perpetrators were speeding away, one of the neighbors identified several digits from the car's license plate and noted the color and make of the vehicle. Jack used his cell phone to call 911 and notify the police that he had just been shot. Because the police detachment is near our home, the police were able to deploy a helicopter and several police cars very quickly. The carload of perpetrators were swiftly apprehended about 1.5 kilometers away by several constables with guns drawn. It was later reported that this incident cost the city nearly a million dollars in resources.

Jack waited about an hour to get a simple surgery and five stitches—he was most fortunate that the pellet had missed his jugular vein, though just barely. But that was the easiest part of the ordeal to get over. Jack managed to join the family for Thanksgiving dinner that night—although he was still emotionally numb—and we most certainly thanked God that nothing *physically* worse had come out of this incident.

I wish I could say the story ended there and we all lived happily ever after. It didn't.

Within a couple of days, Jack broke down in tears, and then he began to express deep hurt and anger over the incident. His emotional condition began to spill over into his other relationships and into his capacity to undertake normal activities. He was having greater difficulties concentrating at school, and he struggled with paranoia when he was walking on the streets, waiting at a bus stop, or taking public transit. It didn't help when students at the school teased him about the ordeal, making their hands into the shape of a gun and pretending to shoot him. I had to drive him to and from school every day. Unfortunately, he still could not cope, and he blew the entire semester at school. School authorities indicated that his post-traumatic stress was more than the school counselors were capable of dealing with. So, Jack was placed into therapy with a specialist who dealt with violent assaults of this nature. This was a very messy season in the life of Jack and in the life of our family.

Jack was so angry, he wanted to legally charge the guys who had shot him. Given the stage of moral development most teens are at, his feelings could be expected.

We were strongly advised to take the route of *restorative justice.* This would mean that Jack (and our family) would face the three perpetrators (and their families) in an extended meeting. The perpetrators would be expected to offer public apologies and do community service. The goal would be to bring some understanding, resolution, closure, and healing to all those involved.

After nearly four months of therapy, some time away from school, and time to reflect, Jack felt he was ready to face the three perpetrators. Even after the end of this process, Jack continued to live with anxiety disorder and post-traumatic stress disorder (PTSD), which further complicated his challenges with ADHD. His emotional well-being had deteriorated, along with some of his behavior at home. He became increasingly oppositional and defiant, though not violent.

Our next big challenge was trying to get Jack back into school after being out for an entire semester. We simply were not successful. And then Jack changed his friends and the company he kept and became involved with another group of kids. Some of these kids had been banned from the school and were engaged in substance abuse. This introduced a new set of problems. In hindsight, my wife and I didn't realize this transition was happening as quickly as we should have, and it would take us a year to come to terms with the fact that Jack was traveling with a different crowd.

Moving On

Eventually, Jack chose to get some training in working security and in operating a forklift. He later was employed providing security and was living in our basement. When Jack turned eighteen, he wanted to go to another province and live and work with his uncle. We tried to change his mind and keep him working locally and going back to school, but he wanted to go. In the back of my mind was the fact that I had savings in a RESP (Registered Education Savings Plan) for our son to eventually get further education.

Jack came back to visit us at Christmas when he was nineteen and then returned to the other province. He eventually moved to another city, where he worked in construction, but he experienced flare-ups and hospitalization due to severe anxiety disorder. He literally could not breathe, and an ambulance had to be called. Our impression from his phone calls was that he wasn't taking good care of himself and his health was compromised. He was challenged with sickness, unemployment, and loneliness. On multiple occasions, we wired him money to help him out.

In the fall of 2012, I was preoccupied with supporting my grandfather in hospice in the final weeks of his life. Out of the blue, Jack phoned, indicating that he was unemployed and he had a girlfriend, Jill,[13] who was pregnant. He pleaded with us for the chance to come and live with us until he could get back on his feet and find work. At the time of that phone call, I remember feeling overwhelmed by the situation, so my wife and I divided up the challenges. I focused on being my grandfather's power of attorney, taking care of his closing estate matters,

---

[13] Again, not her real name.

23

and spending his last dying days with him, while my wife focused on helping Jack and his pregnant girlfriend. I remember feeling very angry with Jack for what I considered to be him living irresponsibly. However, I didn't want to turn my back on him or an unborn grandchild. So, we wired them money for bus fare. They came and stayed in our basement for several months until we could get them the community services they needed and help them rent their own place. There was a lot to process here. I remember feeling very frustrated and overwhelmed because Jack didn't have a good history of taking good care of himself, so how could he care for a wife and a child?

Our granddaughter was born in 2013. I can remember going up to see her, holding her, with Jack, thanking God for the gift of this little life.

I wish I could say that everything went smoothly after this, but it didn't. Over the next year, things would go downhill. Jack and his girlfriend Jill got married in June 2013. We paid for everything pertaining to the wedding and banquet and welcomed a new daughter-in-law into the family. However, they were repeatedly evicted from various residences they rented because of conflicts they got into between themselves and with the landlords. My wife and I tried to be supportive, helped them out with various rental deposits, and even paid the rental of a U-Haul moving truck to help them move. Jack continued to be unemployed during this period. Their continuing crises created significant disruption in our lives. We were always deeply concerned for Jack and his family and found ourselves regularly bringing them groceries or buying things for them. We would eventually realize that there were multiple dynamics going on behind the scenes, including Jack's mother-in-law (Pandora[14]) living with them. Shortly after the birth of our granddaughter Jaded,[15] it was apparent that Jack and Jill's mental health had deteriorated as Jill silently battled postpartum depression. While they were renting a basement suite, Jack had a fall down some concrete stairs and injured his back. He was prescribed oxycodone, an opioid medication, for pain relief. This drew him into a habit. Jack was constantly asking for money for basic things such as milk for the baby. To an experienced social worker, these would be signs that funds were being channeled into an addiction. Eventually, their situation would be unsustainable.

---

[14] Not her real name.
[15] Not her real name.

Chapter 2
Losses and Breakdown

In the summer of 2013, it was alleged by Jack that Jill had taken a whole bottle of pills (a medication called clonazepam) that belonged to Jack. He panicked and called 911, and then Jill bolted out the door. Jack chased after her to try to restrain her. At almost the same time, my wife arrived at their basement suite and discovered the home was a mess. The police arrived and caught up to the two parents. Jill was sent to the hospital, where she spent a week detoxing. We thought that this was just a hiccup in this marriage and these kids would pull their marriage together. Jill's mother, Pandora, would step in to help out in the interim. My wife and I were unable to care for the child, as we were both in highly demanding jobs and our granddaughter at the time was only seven months old and in diapers. However, the child was temporarily removed and placed in a McFamily[16] temporary foster home until transfer to Pandora. We had hoped the kids would quickly get their marriage and family affairs in order. In the meantime, we exercised our grandparent rights and continued to have our granddaughter (Jaded) with us each weekend. Sadly, from 2013 onwards, Jack and Jill both descended into a lifestyle of full-blown substance abuse.

---

[16] I will use this term from this point on to refer to the Ministry that addresses matters pertaining to children and family.

In the spring of 2014, Jack asked if he could live with us in our separate basement space. We tried to help him out, as he was now broken up with his wife. We knew he was hurting badly, and we wanted to give him some support and a sanctuary. He was angry regarding his wife; in his words, he was just trying to restrain her when she was overdosing and running who knows where.

The eight months that our son lived with us were extremely unsettling. Hayslip and Kaminski accurately identify that grandparent caregivers face the double challenge of "coping with their own feelings about an adult child [and] the responsibility of caring for a vulnerable grandchild."[17] Over time, Jack's behavior became more unpredictable and erratic. Both Jack and Jill (who were now back together on their own) became entrenched in their lifestyles and their struggles, and it was necessary for us to keep healthy boundaries for our own well-being.

In the spring of 2015, Jaded was placed in the temporary custody of her maternal grandmother Pandora. I can remember our family attending more than one family case planning conference with McFamily regarding the next steps to be taken— permanency planning (adoption) or moving forward with a 54.1 guardianship order. During this period, between 2015 and 2017, we continued to discuss with McFamily and to consult with lawyers regarding the possibility of joint guardianship or even of adoption. We were uncertain whether to pursue these options through McFamily or through family court. I remember meeting with our first lawyer to discuss

---

[17] Hayslip and Kaminski, "Grandparents Raising their Grandchildren," 266.

adoption. It was very discouraging to hear that the legal fees could reach $50,000 and that we would still risk losing the case because we were not indigenous. That negative probability took all the air out of the room. In those years, we had numerous concerns regarding this child, including lack of supervision, poor hygiene, medical neglect, and poor attendance at daycare. The maternal grandmother/caregiver Pandora often asked my wife for money, and we wondered what was going on. In the start of summer 2017, we received a call saying that Pandora had been found unresponsive. When the police and paramedics arrived, they described the condition of the home as "deeply concerning." The child, Jaded, was removed. It is hard to describe the shock and disappointment we felt.

Chapter 3
Recoveries and Transitions

Some transitions you don't foresee. My wife and I were empty nesters and preparing our portfolio to head into semi-retirement. But all that changed as we were faced with a profoundly difficult decision regarding the future of our biological grandchild Jaded. We contemplated the necessity of becoming parents and primary caregivers again.

In the middle of 2017, my wife called me. She told me that our grandchild was in the hands of McFamily and explained what had happened to make that necessary. We were asked by McFamily if we could take the child. Given our life stage, we believed we could help out with this, utilizing preschool child care. Jaded was then age four. We had to thoughtfully consider how to balance the multiple concurrent roles we had undertaken in order to avoid overload and reduce conflict with our careers.

Researchers have found that one in five skipped generation households contain two or more grandchildren; that the emotional, physical, and economic toll of raising multiple grandchildren is particularly acute; that other relative caregivers (e.g., aunts and cousins) and unrelated foster care providers were less likely than custodial grandparents to be caring for more than one child; and that it is often necessary to split the children up in order to find enough space for them.[18] These are difficult realities to have to face head on.

Our granddaughter Jaded had experienced some distress and came to us with some health issues and anxiety around separation and attachment. She had had quite a number of Adverse Childhood Experiences. She had many questions about her birth parents and maternal grandmother that we answered in an age-appropriate way. We had to address her eating habits because it seemed she previously had been eating too much macaroni and cheese, pizza, coke, and candy, rather than a balanced diet representing the four food groups. We enrolled her in a top-notch daycare, and this enhanced her social skills with her peers and improved her speech. We also started a reading program with our granddaughter, reading a book with her every night and encouraging her to sound out the words. Regular medical and dental checkups were done. We enrolled her in a dance school and theater group, as we discovered she loved to dance and sing. We enrolled her in a swimming class to give her an important survival skill. And we engaged her in cultural activities. We continued to train her and help her develop age-appropriate self-care routines.

We helped our granddaughter attend many cultural events in the community and helped her learn about her mixed cultural heritages. I also enrolled in lectures to further educate myself on indigenous history and culture so as to be more aware and more sensitive to the aboriginal half of her heritage. In the

---

[18] Aron Shlonsky, Barbara Needell, and Daniel Webster, "The ties that bind: A cross-sectional analysis of siblings in foster care," *Journal of Social Services Research*, 29(3), January 2003: 27-52.

process, I reflected on the fact that on both the maternal and paternal sides of my family I had a few First Nations relatives with mixed cultural heritages—an adopted aunt and her children (first cousins) and second cousins. With our granddaughter, we attended aboriginal heritage events such as the Harvest Moon festival and the out of care blanket ceremony. The out of care blanket ceremony was deeply meaningful as it had so much symbolism regarding the transfer of a grandchild to grandparents.

Chapter 4
Fostering: Safe Care

We had been going through various protocols to be able to provide foster care to our granddaughter Jaded, but since 2017 we had also been requesting to adopt the child. This matter was complicated because of the First Nations component, because our granddaughter had a half sibling elsewhere, and because of the need to assess what capacity we had to parent for the next fifteen years, given our stage in life. In the background of our situation was the federal government's focus on reconciliation with First Nations people, which was filtering down into adoption legislation.[19] We were vocal about wanting adoption on the understanding that a permanent decision on providing care for our biological granddaughter would be in the best interest of the child. We decided we wanted to make the commitment to care for our granddaughter until she became an adult, and we asked that custody be transferred to us. By the final month of 2017, we had begun the process of becoming approved restricted foster caregivers. This involved multiple steps that included a home visit, a McFamily prior contact check, and a criminal records search. All of this screening was preliminary to our application to provide foster care. We were provided with the *Foster Family*

---

[19] Government of Canada, "Reducing the number of Indigenous children in care," accessed April 8, 2023: https://www.sac-isc.gc.ca/eng/1541187352297/1541187392851

Handbook: Standards for Foster Homes. We were informed of and adhered to the basic expectations for fostering parents. We understood how important it was to help our granddaughter stay connected to her culture, her family, and her extended family in a positive and respectful manner.

Moving down the road to adoption involved an enormous number of meetings and interviews, endless forms to complete, medical forms to be submitted, a home study to be done, and broader background checks encompassing our economic, marital, psychological, and physical health, our family history, our financial history, and our current financial status. Then there was the intensive seven-module adoption course that involved journaling, testing, and conference calls. If we failed to complete and pass the exams of this adoption course, we would not be able to continue the process. We were both working in demanding jobs at the time, and the only time we had to study the adoption course materials was weeknights and weekends. It was a heavy period and one that had us reflecting a lot on self-care while we were going through the process. As Johnston points out, "The process of adoption is complex, involving many decisions, lots of paperwork, screening and preparation."[20] Throughout all of this, there was always the awareness that at any time McFamily could simply say no to our desire to adopt our biological grandchild.

---

[20] Patricia Irwin Johnston, *Adoption is a Family Affair: What Relatives and Friends Must Know* (London, UK: Jessica Kingsley Publishers, 2012), 16.

Chapter 5
Setbacks and Discrimination

In my discussions with international people from places such as the Philippines, Hong Kong, Asia, and Latin America, I was told that when a child could not be adequately cared for by the birth parents, the child was generally passed into the care of family members, particularly grandparents (a simple transfer within a kin group). However, in Canada, the process of adoption includes legal and inheritance rights, health insurance, and so forth. The process is not simple and involves multiple steps. In our case, we first declared our interest in adopting our granddaughter in 2017 and entered into the next step in the transition—kinship fostering. By late 2019, we had been fostering our granddaughter for two-and-a-half years.

Potential Setback Number 1

At one point, McFamily was considering sending our biological granddaughter to live with an older indigenous couple she was not directly related to, a ferry ride and sixteen hours of travel north of our home—people not part of our granddaughter's biological family group and total strangers to her. My wife attended a McFamily meeting accompanied by her Italian aunt. She commented that her granddaughter also had an Italian family heritage, to which the Anglo lawyer at the table sardonically commented, "Don't worry. We will make sure she gets a plate of pasta." The statement smacked of discrimination against Italians. My wife's father told her that when he came from Italy to Canada, their family frequently received prejudicial treatment from Anglophone and Francophone Canadians, who called them "Wops," and "Degos." The suggestion that a couple who were unknown to our granddaughter and not directly related to her should have a greater priority in providing permanent care for our granddaughter was troubling. It definitely appeared to be placing someone else's needs above the best interest of our granddaughter. The proposed move would rip her away from us and the many other extended family members with whom she had formed attachments and bonded relationships. We were concerned because we had maintained a long-term and extremely stable relationship with our granddaughter since birth. When Jaded was with her birth parents, we had attempted to support them. In our attempt to care for our granddaughter we had made arrangements to have her at our home as much as possible when she was an infant.

After our granddaughter's removal from her birth parents and her placement in foster care and then with her maternal grandmother Pandora, we believed it was important for us to maintain ongoing contact with our granddaughter, and we arranged for her to continue to live with us every weekend. That was a time when we were requesting joint guardianship in planning meetings. Following the removal of our granddaughter from her maternal grandmother Pandora, we, the paternal grandparents, were the only stable adult influence in our four-year-old granddaughter's life. The choices we were faced with were painful and heartbreaking. We had to be realistic regarding what we were capable of taking on.

Being required to complete a full and comprehensive home assessment in order for us to be considered for a restricted foster placement seemed excessive. We felt it did not adequately recognize our biological connection to Jaded as her grandparents, our long-term relationship with her throughout her life, and the attachment between us and our granddaughter which had been ongoing since birth. Our granddaughter was flourishing living with us and was connected with her paternal family in a way that otherwise would not be possible. We were committed to our granddaughter and wanted her to live the best life possible and to become the best possible version of herself.

Sadly, we had to engage the services of yet another lawyer to address this issue of McFamily continuing to search for another placement, no matter how far removed, which would take our granddaughter away from the only stable life she knew. If necessary, we were prepared to initiate a legal process to have the court review the plan of care and determine what was best for our grandchild. We believed a permanency plan with us was in our granddaughter's best interest. In deciding to consult with legal counsel, I remember thinking that this was a critical juncture. We could either back off and let McFamily determine our granddaughter's future— which risked her being placed with another family far away, placing restrictions on us and producing a lot of unforeseen outcomes—or we could exercise our legal rights as biological grandparents. We chose to adopt her, fight to get her out of the system, and raise her within our family, furnishing her with love in the midst of her family circle. If I didn't at least try to adopt her, I didn't think I would be able to look in the mirror twenty years later and feel at peace with myself—especially if our granddaughter's life did not turn out well. We would then have to live with the realization that our granddaughter would feel rejected by us.

The best way I can describe this significant juncture would be by using an analogy from the Christmas movie *It's a Wonderful Life*. In that movie, George Bailey got a chance to see what life would be like if he had never lived. Similarly, we felt like we were being given a chance to see what life would be like if we didn't seek to adopt our granddaughter. George Bailey learned that he wanted to live again, and so did we. We wanted the child to be her best possible self, growing up within her biological family group. Remember that we had only had one child and had always wished we had a second. Well, here was a chance to adopt the daughter we never had—our granddaughter. We wanted her to thrive and flourish, and we wanted to invest in that. This discussion sounds completely rational, but, like most grandparents, we felt these things deep in the core of our hearts.

Potential Setback Number 2

On October 31, 2019, I received an email from the logistics manager at my company saying that there was a meeting in the boardroom with the route sales division salespeople at 6:00 a.m. on November 1 (the next day). It was unconventional for the company to give such a last-minute notice for a sales meeting, but I thought nothing of it. The next morning, I went to the boardroom. The president of the division was there, along with the assistant logistics manager and us salespeople, but there were no donuts and there was no coffee. It was then that I knew this was serious.

One of my colleagues (whose wife had just had a baby in the summer) was the first to go into the boardroom with the two executives. The door was shut. When he came out thirty minutes later, his face was red, and he looked like a deer caught in the headlights. The first thing he said was, "I'm going home."

The president came out, pointed at me, and said, "I will take you next." As we sat down, an envelope was pushed towards me, and a letter was read by the president. Essentially, it stated that the company was changing its business model. The position I had been working in since September 2010 was now redundant because the company was going to take its marketing to online sales and a call center sales format. I was about fifteen minutes into this meeting when it began to hit me that my life was in for an enormous change. The first thing that came to my mind was how this could upset the two-year adoption assessment that was being done on my spouse and me by McFamily, which would be forwarded to the Supreme Court of our province for the adoption. The assessment included questions around whether I had stable employment in the same job. I remembered the social worker asking, "You are not planning on making a job change, are you?" McFamily factored in job stability and steady income in the assessment. At this point, we were just waiting on the government (McFamily) to give us the Notice of Placement, and then, after a six-month waiting period, the matter would go to the Supreme Court, which was the final step to completing the adoption.

After the president had told me that my last day would be November 29 (Black Friday), I was asked if there was anything I wanted to say. I mentioned that I had one concern and that it was regarding how this surprise notice and transition might derail the adoption assessment that was near completion. There was no way I could experience such a profound change and not declare it to McFamily or the courts at this stage of the game.

The logistics manager commented, "I thought that the adoption was already completed."

I stated, "No, it's in the final stages."

The president could have said, "Well that's tough. This is just business." Instead, he said, "Tell me more."

I explained that adoption in Canada is a very lengthy process and that we had been working on it for two years. I commented that when I had applied to join the Vancouver police force, it was about a six-month process. When I had gone to China, acquiring a visa was only a three-month process. But the adoption process had taken two years so far. I noted that I had told both logistics managers back in September that I was just waiting for the Notice of Placement and then I would apply to take two to three months of adoption leave.

My concern, I said, was how this would impact the adoption of our granddaughter, adding, "It's all I can think about right now." I was feeling very emotional at the moment because we had been fighting to get our granddaughter for the last two years and now this was likely to derail it.

The president said, "Well, then. Forget everything I have said to you up to this point. I am taking back the letter right now. I am offering you another job." He described the position and the salary (about $12,000 a year less than my previous position) and asked if I would be willing to accept the terms.

I took the position for the obvious reasons—my problem was solved. I told the president I was touched by the outcome and very grateful.

The president kept apologizing that I was put through what I had just gone through. I was asked if I wanted to take the day off.

I replied, "No. I'm a big boy. I think better when I am working."

I walked out of that meeting feeling as if I had just missed a bullet.

Later in the day, a human resources manager phoned to give me the new job description and commented, "I am so glad they kept you. In the managers' meeting, there was lots of will in the room to keep you because many of the customers really like you, but there was no position for you."

At the end of the day (around 4:00 p.m.) the president came up to me in the parking lot and asked if I was okay. He apologized again for putting me through that meeting.

I responded that I recognized that the company's business model had changed and I was moving forward.

When November 29 (Black Friday) came around, I was offered yet another different job with the company, as a sales representative. Actually, it was a very good fit, given my background education and experience in sales in the marketplace. As strange as it seems, Black Friday became a Good Friday to me. It made me think about why we call Good Friday Good Friday—it represents the intervention and delivery of Good News. That is what had happened for me and my family—an intervention of good news.

However, the offer for the sales representative job was not fulfilled. I had carried over from my previous position a large amount of overtime hours, I was owed statutory holiday hours, and I had vacation time that had not been used yet. In addition, I was taking an adoption leave. The sales department had a small staff and had quotas to meet, and a more senior sales rep was taking a leave. The department could not afford my absence, and so the company rescinded the offer. Nevertheless, I remained with the company, with Operations in supply distribution. I share this story simply to say that yet another potential setback was avoided, and I call this grace. My point is that the needs of our family were covered and protected.

Potential Setback Number 3

On January 28, 2020, we began a six-month adoption placement, which would last until the McFamily paperwork went through the courts to finalize the adoption. During this period, a McFamily social worker (Ms. Encouragement[21]) would visit every month or two.

Our plans were disrupted when China alerted the World Health Organization (WHO) to the presence of an unknown virus in Wuhan, a port city of 11 million people in central Hubei province. I don't think we paid that much attention to the newscast reporting this on December 31, 2019. We were going into the new year of 2020 and feeling good about how things were shaping up. On January 11, China announced the first death from the virus. By January 22, the death toll had jumped up to seventeen, with more than 550 infections. WHO was saying that there was no need for

---

[21] Not her real name.

international concern because they saw no evidence of the virus spreading outside China. However, on January 30, WHO declared the coronavirus a global emergency. By March 7, COVID-19 had killed nearly 3,500 people and infected 102,000 people across more than 90 countries. As a Canadian, I was carefully watching how this was unfolding and the implications that it was having for work and travel. I had a planned trip to Kenya in May with a university, and it didn't look as if it was going to happen. The economy was being hit. Countries were closing their borders. Canada attempted to suppress the spread of COVID-19 so that the health system would not be overwhelmed and lives could be saved. Churches, parks, theaters, and schools were closed. The recreational big band I played in had to cancel rehearsals and engagements because social distancing could not be observed. Our "life group"—a group of eleven adults who met weekly at our home—had to cancel its regular meetings, and we moved to meeting on Zoom. Death and infection rates were announced daily in Canada—by March 26, there were 2,791 cases and 26 deaths. The Canadian dollar fell to a low of 68 cents to the US dollar. Grocery stores experienced food shortages. I literally went through big box stores for seven days to obtain a single package of toilet paper. In hindsight, it is hard to believe that the coronavirus death toll would eventually exceed 7,000,000 worldwide.

One of the impacts of the COVID-19 emergency was that McFamily, lawyers, and the courts were all hit by a shortage of staff. As a result, the courts would only focus on urgent matters—and this impacted the processing and completion of adoptions. In June of 2020, the adoption social worker conducted an interview with our granddaughter, asking what she thought of being adopted (this is done with children over seven years old). This was one of the last steps, and the package of documents for our adoption was set to be submitted to the court in July. But we had no guarantee that COVID would not cause a delay.

During this time, we became aware that other families were also struggling. A number of them had withdrawn from completing adoptions because of the stress the pandemic had put on the economic and relational aspects of those families. Our family felt some of these pressures in regard to our jobs and to our granddaughter not being able to attend school or extracurricular activities with other children. Jaded had a few emotional meltdowns, and we certainly had to adopt some innovative approaches to navigating the external impacts of the COVID-19 pandemic on our family.

Potential Setback Number 4

During the time that the court documents were being delayed due to COVID-19, there was a changeover in the band representative, chief, and council of the First Nations band to which our granddaughter's mother belonged. The former band representative had agreed to the cultural plan we had presented and had consented to our granddaughter's adoption in the last month of 2019. However, in August (after we had completed the six-month adoption placement), the new band representative, chief, and council stated that they would not consent to the adoption unless we added a number of new points to the cultural plan. Those points, in my estimation, were concerning. For example, they were asking us to commit to visit the reserve (in another province) with our granddaughter twice a year. The flight, travel, hotel, meals, and other expenses would be something we would be expected to absorb. Furthermore, they were asking for a once-a-month Zoom conference between an elder and our granddaughter at a cost of $300 per hour (as compensation for the elder's time). In addition, they were asking for a Zoom communication with an elder (at $300 per hour) at every rite of passage of our granddaughter, including when she got her first catamenia. We would also have to pay approximately $250 per year to purchase the Zoom app. We estimated that these extra costs would amount to at least $14,000 annually—at a time when we were moving into our senior years and a period of fixed income. We perceived these requests to be unrealistic, unreasonable, and financially oppressive. As well, my annual vacation time from work would be consumed in fulfilling their requests for visits. It was very frustrating to experience this change, as we thought we had come to an agreement regarding the cultural plan and had done so much to make our granddaughter's First Nations culture a significant element in her daily life. The adoption was delayed as McFamily attempted to work with the band, since the court documents could not be submitted until we had at least tried to negotiate. Trying to get the band to consent to the adoption order stalled the process.

In the eighth month of 2020, we received an email from the adoption worker saying that the First Nations band had canceled a planned meeting with McFamily. The band representative had informed the adoption worker that "They now oppose all adoptions and are claiming they were not included in the planning for the girl." This was in spite of McFamily having many records detailing their attempts to include the band. The band representative stated that they would not participate in a call with an adoption worker present and they would only work with McFamily representatives from the indigenous guardianship team. The whole matter had to be deferred to the adoption manager, the director (Mr. Bureaucrat[22]), and some local elders from their community to make sure that the indigenous guardianship team were aligned in their planning. We were disappointed that this process wasn't more collaborative.

In August 2020, we were asked to make a video to introduce ourselves and our heritages to the band. We found it strange that after almost four years, we were still considered unknown. We were stunned that this late in the process this detailed information—which was already in the hands of McFamily—had not already been shared with the band. The video included statements by us along these lines:

• We acknowledged that we were filming this video on the traditional unceded territory of our local First Nations people group.

• We introduced ourselves as our granddaughter's biological grandparents.

• We included some information about some of the mixed heritage indigenous members in our own extended family (my wife's aunt-in-law, my adopted aunt, and her children.

• We noted how long Jaded had lived with us.

• We explained how she came to live with us.

• We briefly discussed what our granddaughter's struggles were when she came to live with us.

---

22 Not his real name.

• We described how our granddaughter was doing now.

• We described how we were intentional in helping our granddaughter gain an appreciation for her indigenous culture and stated that it was important to us that she would grow up knowing her culture.

• We stated how much we loved and cared for our granddaughter.

• We included a video of some of the indigenous art in our home and a video of our granddaughter showing some of her indigenous jewelry and books.

The meeting that was supposed to happen in the fall of 2020 between the adoption representatives in our province and the band in the other province never happened. We continued to wait uneasily as the adoption process dragged on with no apparent closure in sight. Although we tried to keep this matter away from our granddaughter, I suspect she picked up on it by overhearing us in a phone call or in conversation.[23]

In mid-autumn 2020, we received an email from our adoption social worker, Ms. Encouragement, regarding a conversation the director (Mr. Bureaucrat) and a team leader had had with the band

---

[23] An unusual matter came up around this. On Saturday, we had been talking around the breakfast table about dreams. Our granddaughter matter-of-factly said that she had seen God in a dream. She was walking and came closer to God, and felt good. Then, she heard God say to her, "It will be well with you." That sounded very articulate and detailed for a seven-year-old. The next day, Sunday, my wife and I channel surfed into a TV program that happened to land upon the topic of "hearing God." It mentioned that God speaks through dreams. I pondered the thought: Had our granddaughter described a dream of wishful thinking regarding the adoption, or was there something more here—was this one of those unexplainable moments?

representative. The email said the band leaders "are very supportive of your granddaughter being in your care and remaining in your care. They agree that the best place for her is with you both." However, the band expressed discomfort with the legal term "adoption." The band was working to develop tribal laws around adoption, but they were not in place yet. The band wanted McFamily to change from adoption to 54.1 (transfer of guardianship)—that is, our granddaughter would remain in the custody of the government, but the government would transfer guardianship to us. The director (Mr. Bureaucrat) and team leaders (Ms. Heartless and Ms. P.C.[24]) explained the differences between the two options in our province and said that there would be no services available through the guardianship option. The band did not know this, as guardianship in their province was almost identical to adoption in terms of services. In the end, the band representative said that she would meet with the chief and council regarding adoption. Their next meeting would be in a month, in January 2020. She also stated that the band would want to see "a lot more detail" put into our granddaughter's cultural plan. Ms. Encouragement advised us, "We may need to be flexible in that area to keep things moving." She also said that the director (Mr. Bureaucrat) would talk to the band representative again in the third week of October and would be working to prepare a formal briefing. He wondered if we had any family photos we might feel comfortable sharing in the briefing. The email concluded, "I hope you have a restful Thanksgiving."

---

[24] Not their real names.

In response, we thanked Ms. Encouragement for the update and sent some photos. However, I took issue with the band's demand that "a lot more detail" needed to be added to our granddaughter's cultural plan. I said, "This feels like 'death by a thousand cuts,' as the bar has been set so high...My sense was that we already *exceeded* the standard demands on a cultural agreement...It feels somewhat oppressive and exacting, a moving of the goalposts, trying to make things as difficult as possible. I feel there is the absence of 'good will' and being fair." I noted that the band's previous demands could cost us about $14,000 a year, demands that were "completely unrealistic and unreasonable for us moving soon into our retirement chapter of life." I said that this was unfair since we were the biological grandparents and were actively seeking to serve her developmental needs while the other party had given absolutely nothing...except inflated demands. I also stated that we had reached out to a child advocacy agency to advocate on behalf of our granddaughter in regards to the apparent stalling of McFamily in processing the adoption through the courts. It appeared that McFamily was uncomfortable with the optics of the situation and had chosen to follow a new political course in keeping with the federal government's efforts to advance reconciliation with First Nations groups. I said, "Our granddaughter deserves to have a 'forever home,' and has a right to be with her blood kin and be given legal rights of inheritance."

Potential Setback Number 5

On November 9, 2020, my wife reported back to work after her government-protected adoption leave. She had been with a management team since 2006 (fourteen years) and had helped to set up and develop the department.

At the time she had submitted her request for adoption leave, she had followed all governmental requirements and given her manager two months' notice. She had gone to the benefits department before requesting leave and asked if there were risks. She said she was afraid of retaliation for requesting an adoption leave, and they said, "No, that wouldn't happen." However, when she put in for the adoption leave, she experienced a very negative vibe coming from her manager. The manager was frustrated that she would have to reallocate my wife's work, so my wife gave up extra time to show her how to perform one of her usual tasks.

On the first day of my wife's leave, she noticed that her access to payroll and other management information at the hospital where she worked had been deleted. She followed up on this, and the payroll department traced the deletion to her supervisor. While my wife was away, her position was filled by a department clerk who was paid about half the salary my wife had received. During the pandemic, organizations were trying to save money on budgets, and payroll was one of the areas where they thought they could make cuts.

When my wife returned to work at 8:00 a.m. on Monday, November 9, she was greeted by other employees. She unpacked her stuff, got a cup of coffee, and greeted some others. She waved to her supervisor, but the supervisor did not acknowledge her. Then the supervisor came to her desk, asked if she had been successful in accessing the computer drives, but said she did not think her email access would be restored that day. Then the Accounts Receivable (AR) manager came to have a casual conversation about COVID and other matters. At 8:30, the supervisor called her into a staff meeting.

After only about ten minutes, the AR manager said, "I need to interrupt. I need Ms. Hopeful to come with me for a moment." My wife was taken to another conference room and was introduced to the director of compensation and management services for the hospital. The AR manager said, "We have decided to terminate your employment with us as of today." This came as a surprise. My wife's last performance review had been very positive, and she had been given a raise—you don't give people raises for bad performance. The issue was clearly not her performance, but retaliation for taking an adoption leave. The AR manager promptly left the room, and the director of compensation and management began to discuss her severance package.

In retrospect, my wife recognized that neither her supervisor nor the AR manager had been happy about her request for "government protected" adoption leave from the beginning. The pandemic had made things more difficult for the organization, and she felt that some of that was being projected onto her. During the pandemic, many organizations engaged in heavy-handed layoffs using various excuses. The timing was bad for the organization. But government rules meant that adoption parental leave had to be taken within a limited time of the placement of adoption or it would be forfeited.

Not only did my wife understand that her termination was unjust and a form of retaliation for taking a leave. She also found that the whole game of being received back in the office only to be terminated was humiliating and embarrassing. She had been ushered out the side door like a common thief. As well, she believed that she had been let go because of her age so that they could hire someone younger and for less money to save the department money. This was targeted age discrimination. After fourteen years in that job, she was being thrust into a job market that was already prejudiced against older workers. Due to being fired, her chances of being able to break back into the marketplace were diminished, especially during the COVID-19 pandemic when millions were unemployed and the competition was fierce. This was especially galling because fourteen years earlier she had been recruited for this position and had given up a career elsewhere to take the job. In sum, the whole situation caused a lot of stress and anxiety.

My wife's next step was to consult an employment rights lawyer, who concluded that there had been four human rights violations in my wife's "no fault termination." My wife communicated this to the director of compensation and management services. She stated, "From my meeting with the lawyer, I understand that a leave of absence to care for an adopted child is a job-protected leave under the Employment Standards Act and I cannot be terminated because of this. I was told that the Employment Standards Tribunal has power to reinstate me or order compensation so that I can be 'made whole.' The lawyer also told me that if any part of the reason for my termination was related to my age or family status, I could bring a human rights complaint for discrimination and seek injury to dignity damages on top of wage loss."

We have concluded that people who take adoption leaves are highly discriminated against in a marketplace that sees workers as a commodity.

Adoption leaves should be as protected as maternity leaves, but it is clear that organizational lawyers have found ways to get around such requirements and put gag orders on employees who experience forms of discrimination such as we experienced. As my wife discovered, even if you take legal recourse, the recovery for discriminatory damages is miniscule—we were notified that my wife would be lucky to recover $5,000. The laws seem to be written to protect organizations, not workers. The laws around adoption leaves and attitudes in the general public towards alternative families[25] are in need of change. When you read the government description of these laws, the public is led to believe that you are protected, but in our experience, people in situations such as ours are profoundly vulnerable to retaliation in the workplace. It can be the end of your career or being passed up for a promotion.

---

[25] Alternative families include grandparents parenting, single parents, co-parents, and same-sex parents.

Chapter 6
Reflections on
the First Summit

In the last month of 2020, our adoption placement had been ongoing for nearly eleven months. Adoption placement is only supposed to last six months, and then the adoption goes to the court. In the Christmas month, we received notification that the adoption social worker (Ms. Encouragement) had been removed from involvement with the band and our file had been moved to the management team.

I followed up, sending emails to the adoption team leader, the director (Mr. Bureaucrat), and the other director (Ms. Heartless). In essence, I wrote: "We are the grandparents of Jaded. Our granddaughter has resided with us for several years and was placed for adoption with us in the first month of 2020. We finished our placement requirements by the summer of 2020. Then, we were advised of a misunderstanding between McFamily and the band. In the last month of 2019, the band representative had agreed to the cultural plan agreement that had been drawn up. Yet, when it came time to sign the papers and move forward to the courts, McFamily tried several times to obtain the signed documents. When they finally connected, our worker found out that there is now a new band representative who apparently put forth a new agreement and disagrees with the adoption placement of the former chief and council. We were advised that this matter is no longer in the hands of our adoption social worker and has moved up to your attention. There apparently have been some conversations with the band representative, and we were advised that the representative would speak to the band council and contact McFamily with an update. We also understand that the child advocate agency has advised that McFamily has a legal right to proceed with submitting the adoption to the courts without the band's approval. We have signed the original cultural agreement, and, through no fault of our own, there has been an unprecedented placement extension. We are at the point that January 2021 will mark one year of waiting. How much longer will you wait? What are you waiting for before proceeding with the final step? We would like you to provide us with a definite date when you will put the waiting to an end and proceed with signing the papers for the courts."

In the third week of December 2020, I received one email response, from the director (Mr. Bureaucrat). It was pleasant, including an apology for the delay in responding to my email and acknowledging "how difficult this delay must be for your family." It further stated, "I have confirmed that a McFamily representative was in contact with the band at the end of last week to request an update. Although I understand that you would like a definite date when McFamily will put the waiting to an end and proceed with signing of the papers for the courts, I do not have a specific date. However, I do remain hopeful that our continuing communication with the band will provide a response shortly."

As we reached the end of the year, we considered our options. We could file a formal complaint with McFamily, asking for a review of why the adoption placement had been extended so long. (This would turn out to be a waste of time because the review process was just a lower department under those who make the real decisions and it would be like asking an employee to tell the boss what to do.) We could reach out to our local MLA. We could also reach out to our lawyer to draft a letter and move forward with a legal process.

In the first month of 2021, our adoption social worker (Ms. Encouragement) notified us that she had received no update from management regarding the First Nations band's position. We also learned that the child advocacy agency had inquired again regarding our granddaughter's situation. Because this matter had dragged on for so long, we would now have to provide an annual update to our granddaughter's' care plan.

In the second month of 2021, we received an email saying that the band chief and council would be meeting in the next week to give a final answer. Therefore, the director (Mr. Bureaucrat) wanted to schedule a meeting with my wife and me, the director, and the other director (Ms. P.C.) to share the band's decision. We were told, "You are welcome to invite anyone else who you might wish to bring as an advocate." We considered this last point a very significant statement, implying that we might not be happy with the decision.

In preparation for the meeting, I had booked the day off work using my vacation time. I reflected that I had had to use a lot of vacation time for meetings with McFamily. I also reflected on how costly this whole adoption process had been. My wife and I had spent many hours in meetings, filling out documents, sending and receiving emails, talking on the phone, networking, interacting with various agencies, and rescheduling our lives in order to discuss matters pertaining to our granddaughter. There were also additional costs involved in needing to have our lawyer present. Our granddaughter was only six months old when we had first become involved with McFamily, at first advocating for joint guardianship with the maternal grandmother Pandora. By the time our granddaughter was four, we had requested and begun working to adopt her. She was now eight years old—and still in the system. After four intense years, we were exhausted by the whole process. And yet what needed to be done in "the best interest of the child" was clearly obvious.

The Meeting

The first mid-morning meeting took place and included three McFamily directors, a McFamily lawyer (Mr. Casuistic), the adoption social worker (Ms. Encouragement), a children's advocate (Ms. Compassionate), our lawyer (Ms. Noble),[26] and my wife and me. The children's advocate was there for our granddaughter, to fight for the child's best interest. This meeting was done on Skype, with just blank boxes and no facial images, so we could only hear voices—a very impersonal, detached, and cold choice for a meeting dealing with intimate family relationships. Following is a reflective summary and overview of the interactions between the various participants in the meeting:

Everything should have been going routinely, McFamily was following a particular process, and they were careful in what they were doing. However, they

---

26 Again, these are not their real names.

didn't tell us, or clearly explain, that what they were doing involved a technical change whereby at the last step they would try to pull the rug out from under us. The meeting began with the adoption social worker Ms. Encouragement outlining the background of the case: acceptance of my wife and me as restricted foster parents in 2017, beginning of the adoption process in 2018, approval of the adoption process in the ninth month of 2019, communications from the First Nations band implying the band approved of adoption in December 2019, adoption placement in January 2020, a new band council saying they did not approve of the adoption in July 2021, and extension of the adoption placement until the third week of March 2021.

I can briefly summarize my experience of it as follows: The directors Mr. Bureaucrat and Ms. P.C. indicated that for the last several months they had had numerous communications with the band and they supported the band's request for a 54.1 guardianship. It was indicated that the band would not support adoption because of "the 60's scoop" (the adoption of a large number of indigenous children by non-indigenous parents in the 1960s), the history of colonialism, and the federal government's Truth and Reconciliation mandate—all political reasons. The directors wanted to acknowledge the connection of the band with our granddaughter. Ms. P.C. indicated that McFamily supported our home being our granddaughter's permanent home (since we were her family), but only under the 54.1 guardianship option, not adoption. She explained that the band was in the process of creating self-government for itself and viewed adoption as a colonially imposed process. We were told that the First Nation's opposition to adoption was not directed at us (even though we would be the ones directly impacted by it) and they simply could not support adoption based on their history with the government, particularly the federal government (which had nothing to do with our adoption process). The director stated that their position on adoption for children who were half indigenous was based on McFamily policy and new legislation by the federal government. McFamily wanted to support the First Nation in their decision and to help us see their viewpoint. It was made clear to us that if we decided to take the adoption to court, McFamily would oppose us. We were also told that there were only three options on the table, which were:

1. Continuing Custody Order (CCO) status—our granddaughter would remain in McFamily's custody.

2. 54.1 guardianship—our granddaughter would remain in the custody of McFamily, but McFamily would transfer guardianship to us.

3. The First Nation could ask for a reassessment of our granddaughter being placed with us—if we refused either of the first two options, there was a risk we would lose custody of our granddaughter altogether.

In the midst of this hard news, McFamily reiterated that they fully supported the guardianship option. The planning struck us as having been done insufficiently, and the possibility of reassessment was shocking—it felt like a threat. We were in shock over a completely different, large decision to be made. Meanwhile, one of the McFamily team stated that "we should celebrate that the band would like the granddaughter to remain with Mr. and Mrs. Hopeful." We were keenly aware that the band had had no involvement with the child's life up to this eight-year point. We needed to consult our lawyer.

The government and McFamily were displaying professionalism and an intent to look at the best interest of the child, which included exposure to traditional culture. But it also seemed clear to me that they were being supportive of a cultural system that was obstructing non-indigenous blood family members from adopting their own kin with a mixed cultural heritage. I considered this an unjust practice, a problematic policy, and an inappropriate way of proceeding. It manifested prejudice, and I suggested that two wrongs do not make a right. I added that situations such as ours "test the integrity of the Canadian system," which should focus on "the best interest of the child." That the band in this case would stonewall adoption it seemed to me was about other issues, not the best interest of the child. That McFamily had wrestled over the optics of this matter seemed also not to be about the best interest of the child. After seven-and-a-half years, McFamily was still struggling with this matter when the solution we had offered to adopt her was simple and clearly in her best interest. I wondered how many other children with a mixed cultural heritage had been caught in a similar scenario. I questioned if all of the social media advertising that McFamily does encouraging adoption was a misrepresentation—showing pictures of children with mixed cultural heritage needing to be adopted but not informing the public that non-indigenous blood-related people need not apply. I suggested that the process for non-indigenous people to adopt their own half indigenous relatives required the kind of effort needed to climb Mount Everest. What needed to be done was obvious and simple, but

McFamily was not seeing it. McFamily had decided to oppose the adoption—we felt the facts were clear. I asked how the government could turn its back on families wanting to adopt biologically related children with a mixed cultural heritage—refusing them because of their race and ethnicity? I wondered, "Would they do this to Afro-Canadian, Indo-Canadian, or Asian-Canadian grandparents?" The jury is out on this question.

By this point, my wife was in tears, heartbroken that a bureaucratic decision (informed by the federal governments former colonial practices to assimilate First Nations) about our granddaughter's future was being made by a group of people who had never seen the child. Our tears and our words fell on deaf ears as the McFamily director Mr. Bureaucrat responded coldly, "Best to speak with your legal counsel."

Another problem addressed was the absence of contact from the band with the child. The overtures my wife and I had made to our grandchild's maternal family had been many and had not been reciprocated. In contrast, we had always been involved in the child's life in every meaningful way.

Part of our granddaughter's sense of self-identity was growing out of her relationship with her grandparents, and so the question was, "How can the band that had had no contact with the child have such a detrimental impact on her that would change the rest of her life?"

I had many questions: How was this decision made in our granddaughter's best interest? Who would now tell our granddaughter Jaded that she was not adopted? Would we tell her we were just kidding? Earlier, there had been an adoption placement celebration party led by two social workers from

McFamily, where documents were signed, pictures taken, and adoption gifts given to the child. What were the photographs, the chalkboard that said, "Happy Adoption," and the gifts from adoption social workers all about if they weren't saying, "You are now adopted by your grandparents?" What had been the point of signing the adoption papers thirteen months ago? What about the adoption placement that was now being scrapped? How could McFamily simply disregard all of the legal steps that had already been taken? How could they just pull the rug out from under us? My wife noted, "With a 54.1 guardianship, our granddaughter will not have a forever home or inheritance rights unless we specifically put her in our will." Throughout the discussion, it was obvious there were gaps in McFamily's logic. Another meeting had to be set. The adoption social worker (Ms. Encouragement) reminded us that the adoption placement would soon expire, which put pressure on us to decide for 54.1 guardianship or fostering or face the risk of reassessment.

Summary Understanding of the Meeting

We left this first meeting with the McFamily directors feeling shocked, stunned, and hurt by what felt like a "bait and switch" experience. We felt we had been assured of one thing (adoption) and had been given something much less. At the conclusion of the meeting, my wife was holding her head in her hands and weeping. McFamily was pressuring us to accept 54.1 guardianship. This would require us to comply with a set of new orders and a brand new, ever evolving cultural plan that McFamily would put in place, dismissing the previous cultural plan that had already been agreed to by a former band chief and council. It was shocking that the band was allowed to have this level of decision-making power when the band had no relationship with the child. We realized that McFamily held all the power, they were firmly opposed to adoption, and they were strongly pressuring us to accept their decision. Despite the professionalism, integrity, and intention to look at the best interest of the child, in my opinion this file had been bungled largely to placate the band and to follow government political policy—to try to achieve reconciliation and right an historic wrong in the government's colonial history of assimilating First Nations).

We basically had two options. When the adoption placement terminated, we could accept the transfer to 54.1 guardianship. But this would mean that our granddaughter could never be adopted. She would never be able to be adopted by her non-indigenous side of the family. She would lose the right—a right non-indigenous children do not lose—to be adopted by her own biological relatives. Alternatively, we could go to court. How successful this would be might depend on how contentious McFamily would become. The optics would be horrible for McFamily, which is why I suspect they were hoping we would back down. However, if McFamily chose to throw money at this case, we knew we were in no position to match the government's deep pockets. (The thought of this was too grievous to think about, that the system and its practices could potentially be bent this way.) On the other hand, if McFamily chose to leave the matter alone, we could quietly apply to the court on our own. It would then be up to the court to decide the case, and we hoped the court would focus on what was in the child's best interest.

The risk was that we could not know which judge would be assigned to the case or how that judge would decide. If the judge did not side with adoption, we would likely be viewed with disfavor by McFamily, and the threat of "reassessment" could become actual.

When we received the minutes from the first summit meeting, there were a couple of things that were different from what we thought had been discussed in the meeting. First, it became clear that the 54.1 guardianship was still just a proposal that could be declined. Second was the statement "the Nation could ask for a reassessment of placement for the child under federal legislation as the child is still a CCO" (that is, under a Continuing Custody Order). It was made clear that if we didn't go along with the guardianship option, the child could be reassessed for placement and removed from our family. Furthermore, we had been told the band was creating a brand new, ongoing, evolving cultural plan we would have to comply with.

Despite the fact that social workers in various departments had affirmed we had met all the criteria to complete the adoption in court, everything was being stripped back to a basic foster placement with kin (us), with no permanency plan for the child. There had been no permanency plan for seven-and-a-half years of this child's life. And it appeared that even the foster placement was vulnerable, subject to change.

Our granddaughter had had her right to be adopted by her biological family on her paternal side stripped away by the director. This concluding decision had been made because of the colonial history of the federal government. The government was trying to correct its historic assimilation practices without fully considering the best interest of the child.

The decision had been made by two powerful parties (McFamily and the band) that had never even seen the child, and yet that decision would impact the rest of her life. With the last day of the third month being the day when her status would revert to Child Custody Order fostering, with McFamily working on a new cultural plan, and with 54.1 guardianship being "just a proposal," we were rightly concerned. Our best guess was that the completion of a new cultural plan would take many months. Given the fact that obtaining an answer on the adoption proposal had taken thirteen months, we had no idea how long it would take for the chief and band council to reply to the director's proposal for 54.1 guardianship. Further, we were aware that the proposal could be ignored or simply declined, as it carried no weight. At the stroke of a pen, all of the work done towards adoption had been scrapped. At the stroke of a pen, a child would be trapped in the McFamily system under a Child Custody Order. At the stroke of a pen, a child had had her right to be adopted robbed from her.

Chapter 7
Reflections on
the Second Summit

The second meeting took place approximately one month later, with thirteen people present—nine from McFamily (including a higher-level director), one government child advocate, and my wife and me with our lawyer on Skype in an office. The meeting did not go well. The pressure was on. McFamily simply dug their heels in deeper in support of the band's position that the child could not be adopted by her biological grandparents. A summary of my memory of the interaction follows:

The band would only support 54.1 guardianship. They had committed to have the children returned to the Nation. It was noted that this "goes back to colonial issues." (This illustrated again that the decision was being made because of the colonial and political history the band had had with the Canadian government.)

For us, a big issue with guardianship was the problem of "aging out" (that is, when a child in the care of McFamily reaches nineteen, all support for the child ceases). We recognized that the strongest placement of a child is the healthiest, but it appeared that this decision was made to support the band. The child was eight years old, and it was hard for us to understand why the band, which had no connection with the child, would have the final say. We had done everything we could to try to reach out to the band, including forwarding pictures and a video through a McFamily representative. A cultural plan had been completed and approved before the adoption placement. We were made to understand that the band now wanted an evolving cultural plan that could continue to be added to. It struck me that there were burdensome implications in what was now being asked for. Prior to our adoption placement, consultation with the first band council had been done as required. A full safe assessment had been completed by the guardian team. However, a new band council had taken a very different position, and McFamily wanted to go with the band's position.

There had never been any active band involvement with the child; notably, nobody from the band was even involved in these summit discussions. So, the question was: "Where is the child's best interest?" People who spoke from McFamily could not speak beyond the political factors around the child's best interest. One McFamily representative (Ms. Heartless) talked about the politics of the situation, saying, "Adoption isn't something in the First Nations culture." (It occurred to me this might not have been a wholly accurate statement.[27]) I was struck by the comments of an advocate at the summit (Ms. Compassionate) who said, "My concern is, in trying to hold this child in this community, if they are not actually pushing her away from it by what they are

---

[27] "The practice of adopting individuals into one's family has been practiced by all First Nations since time immemorial." Legal Affairs and Justice, "Adoption and Indian Registration," accessed January 14, 2025: https://www.afn.ca/wp-content/uploads/2020/01/17-19-02-06-AFN-Fact-Sheet-Adoption-and-Indian-Registration-final-revised.pdf

doing. This potentially could alter the relationship for her and for future generations. How did the band commit to this child? How is this relationship building, rather than relationship destroying?"

One McFamily representative (Ms. Heartless) talked at some length about the colonial reasons why McFamily wouldn't consent to a mixed cultural heritage child being adopted by her non-indigenous biological grandparents. The executive director confessed, "I made the final decision that the child could not be adopted."

I said, "I have just one simple question: Does a child have a right to be adopted, yes or no?" There was dead silence among the nine McFamily representatives in the meeting. I asked the question a second time. There was silence again, and then Ms. Heartless, raising her voice, said that they were supporting the band. It became very clear to us that this had to go to court.

Summary Understanding of the Meeting

It was clear that the McFamily directors and the band, who had never ever met the child, were making decisions that would profoundly impact the rest of Jaded's life. Although it might be hard to prove that the directors acted unreasonably, it was blatantly obvious to some of us in the meeting that they were not wholly keeping their focus on acting "in the best interest of the child."

It was clear that my wife and I needed to quickly file a petition to the Supreme Court, as, according to the legislation, we had only a short window to apply to adopt before the adoption placement expired. It was clear McFamily were not going to change their decision, and in court the director would have to explain to a judge why her political decision (based on more recent government mandates) was in the best interest of the child. It would also force the band to provide proof of what they had done for the child over the last eight years. This petition would also need to request an extension of the adoption placement until the case was finalized in court.

Chapter 8
Reflections on
the Supreme Court Hearing

We had only three weeks to get an adoption petition in to the provincial Supreme Court. Otherwise, the adoption placement would expire, and our granddaughter would be moved back into foster care, making it very difficult for us to seek adoption at the court level.

We filed a petition to adopt Jaded under section 35(1) of the Adoption Act. The facts of the case were clear. McFamily's top director, Ms. Heartless, did not know Jaded, nor had the band Jaded's mother was from made any attempt to contact her or otherwise engage with her throughout her life. Ms. Heartless (from McFamily) had formerly issued a positive pre-adoption assessment report approving our request to adopt our granddaughter. The pre-adoption assessment report included a cultural plan of care approved by the band. The top director's delegates had told Jaded that she had been adopted by us, and she had arranged for us and Jaded to sign a certificate confirming Jaded's adoption. However, Ms. Heartless had not submitted Jaded's adoption application to the court after approving our application to adopt Jaded and completing the post-adoption placement assessment. Meanwhile, the band's governance had changed. Ms. Heartless had extended the placement for adoption with us, and her delegate had advised us that the top director still supported Jaded's placement for adoption with us. The phone call from McFamily's delegates telling us that they would not proceed with the adoption because of the band's new position on adoption was a game changer. Ms. Heartless would now allow the adoption placement of Jaded with us to expire, which would cause irreparable prejudice to us and, in our view, would be contrary to the best interest of Jaded. We were concerned that Ms. Heartless was not acting in the child's best interest in determining her plan of care. Our petition argued that McFamily director Ms. Heartless was not acting in the best interest of the child because she had initially approved our adoption application; had delayed filing the adoption application past the six-month time period when adoptions are typically filed; had extended the adoption placement while representing to us that our adoption application continued to be approved; had withdrawn approval of our adoption application thirteen months later because of a second consultation with a new governing band council; was aware that the band had never had contact with the child during her lifetime; was aware that Jaded wanted to be adopted by her biological grandparents; knew that Jaded believed she had been adopted by us; was willing to allow Jaded to suffer because a previous decision had been changed by a group of people who were elected every two years and who did not have any personal connection to the child.

Therefore, we sought an order requesting that McFamily's consent to the adoption be dispensed with and that the Supreme Court grant us the right to adopt our granddaughter.

McFamily obtained a lawyer to fight against our petition to adopt our own biological grandchild. It is our conviction that this case should never have had to go to court, but it had become bogged down over politics (historic colonial matters) instead of being about "the best interest of the child." There were two court sessions. I can summarize that they concluded with McFamily signing off on the documents for the adoption to be processed as a "petitioned and contested adoption."

For four weeks, McFamily involved various departments to try to get us to agree to a "wish list" of additional cultural requirements that we would have to carry out beyond the original cultural agreement we had completed.

Finally, in the middle of 2021, the adoption order was signed by the lawyers and the Supreme Court judge. Exactly four years to the day Jaded had come to live with us full time, her adoption was settled and permanent.

Chapter 9
Reflections on the Process

Our experience in attempting to adopt our granddaughter convinced us that the system (how McFamily and similar agencies process children with a mixed cultural heritage) is in need of revision. We discovered during our adoption journey that First Nations children under age 14 represented about 7.7% of the children in Canada but about 53.8% of the children under 14 in the foster care system.[28] Furthermore, it has anecdotally come to my attention that many First Nations bands refuse to allow non-indigenous grandparents, aunts, uncles, and other relatives to adopt children who have a mixed cultural heritage. Their preference is for First Nations relatives to have priority to be foster parents, guardians, and adoptive parents. This gives First Nations bands the upper hand in determining which family a child of mixed heritage is placed with. Fostering and guardianship come with government money to help meet the child's needs. However, adoption changes this financial support. My point is that adoption is not about obtaining financial help. It is about *love for the child* and providing a forever family (true permanence and care). Government should be aware that the system and process of

---

[28] Government of Canada, "Reducing the number of Indigenous children in care," accessed January 13, 2025: https://www.sac-isc.gc.ca/eng/1541187352297/1541187392851

adoption for mixed heritage children currently hinders non-indigenous biological family members from adopting their part-indigenous kin. This, in my view, is a biased practice. Agencies such as McFamily need to be held accountable for their decision making. The issue of familial adoption of mixed heritage children should be looked at very closely because some bands' policies block such adoptions that provide true permanency and care; people related to the child should not be taken away from the child. This is an area that needs judicial oversight outside of the politicized bureaucracy of McFamily. Blocking non-indigenous family members who want to adopt their mixed heritage kin represents a form of prejudice and discrimination. Two wrongs do not make a right.[29] My wife and I have the sense that we are part of a small percentage of grandparents (and other family kin) who have requested adoption instead of guardianship. I suspect that there are a lot of families that don't even get this far in this highly politicized system. These requests test the integrity of McFamily's administrative scheme and whether it wholly operates in *the best interest of the child*. That the band would obstruct an adoption based on historic colonial issues likely demonstrates that it was not wholly acting in the best interest of the child. That McFamily might have been concerned with the optics of this matter likely demonstrates that it was not wholly acting in the best interest of the child. That

---

[29] What I mean by saying "Two wrongs don't make a right" is that just because the federal government acted prejudicially toward First Nations peoples in the history of Canada doesn't make it right for ministries to now act prejudicially toward another racial people group—as if a current wrong can somehow make up for an historical wrong.

McFamily was still taking this approach seven-and-a-half years later, when the solution we offered to adopt our granddaughter was simple and straightforward, demonstrates that it was not wholly acting in the best interest of the child.

I have wondered how many other children with a mixed cultural heritage have been trapped in the system, losing their right to be adopted by non-indigenous biological relatives. I have questioned how much of the social media advertising that McFamily does to encourage adoption could be a form of misrepresentation—showing pictures of mixed indigenous children who are needing to be adopted but not informing the public that, for the majority of these children, non-indigenous people need not apply. The process for non-indigenous kin to adopt their own mixed heritage relatives may require the kind of effort needed to climb Mount Kilimanjaro—that is, taking the matter to the Supreme Court at their own expense. For many, adoption may be unattainable because of their ethnicity.

This is a serious issue. About 250,000 adoptions happen every year worldwide. In Canada, about 20,000 children are permanent wards of the state, meaning a bureaucracy is their legal guardian.[30] By the time they reach age nineteen, they will "age out" without an adopted family to catch them, including the provision of rights to inheritance. "Each year, only about 1,200 children become adopted, giving them homes. Meanwhile, Canadians adopt about 2,000

[30] Leslie Papp, Tanya Talaga, and Jim Rankin, CYCNET, "Feature: Nobody's Children," accessed October 10, 2021: https://cyc-net.org/features/ft-nobody'schildren.html

children a year from outside the country."[31] My wife and I were exhausted from the long adoption process and the unnecessary tension it introduced into our family. There is something very wrong with McFamily stopping the adoption of mixed race First Nations children by their non-indigenous relatives. People in my country make a big deal about countries that block the rights of children (such as, Sierra Leone, Chad, and Central African Republic) or the rights of women (such as, Pakistan, Somalia, Sudan, and especially Afghanistan, where half the population—women, and female children—are legally restricted from obtaining an education and effectively participating in their nation's economic well-being). Yet little attention is paid to a problem we have in Canada, where half of a mixed heritage indigenous child's family (the non-indigenous half, whether black, Caucasian, Asian, or some other race and ethnicity) can find themselves restricted or gridlocked from adopting their biological kin. Removing these restrictions could effectively bring down the number of mixed heritage children trapped in the foster care system. There are an astounding number of these children in care.[32] As

---

[31] Leslie Papp, Tanya Talaga, and Jim Rankin, CYCNET, Canada: "More than 20,000 await adoption, but most remain wards of the state" (October 4, 2001), accessed October 10, 2021: https://cyc-net.org/profession/readarounds/ra-papp.html.
Ipsos tracking reveals that these statistics continue to be consistent over time: Ipsos, "Adoption in Canada," accessed April 9, 2023:
https://www.ipsos.com/en-ca/adoption-canada#:~:text=There%20are%20currently%20more%20than,who%20were%20adopted%20in%20Canada.
[32] Government of British Columbia, "Children and Youth in Care, Case Data and Trends," accessed July 4, 2021: https://mcfd.gov.bc.ca/reporting/services/child-

stated before, First Nation's children under 14 only make up 7.7% of all Canadian children. In 2011, 30% of the children in the foster care system were full or partial First Nations children. In 2021, when we were in court to adopt our granddaughter, 53.8% of the children under age 14 in the foster care system were full or partial First Nations children. The problem is escalating progressively, and partly, I would argue, because of the inordinate focus on indigenous heritage for mixed heritage children and how that can overrule being adopted.[33] With First Nations children under age 14 making up 53.8% of those in the foster care system,[34] something is very wrong with the system when family members can only finalize an adoption that would be in the best interest of a child by taking the matter to the provincial Supreme Court through the Family Law Act. My wife and I have a couple of financially well-off and well-educated Chinese-Canadian friends who were infertile. They wanted to adopt a First Nations child but chose an international adoption because they had heard from other friends the challenges with attempting to adopt a First Nations child in Canada.

Again, I want to argue that the issue of familial adoption of mixed heritage children should be looked at very closely because some bands' policies impede

---

protection/permanency-for-children-and-youth/performance-indicators/children-in-care

[33] See: Laura Kane, "Indigenous heritage doesn't overrule other factors in adoption: B.C. Court" (CTV News, August 9, 2017).

[34] Government of Canada, "Reducing the number of indigenous children in care," accessed April 8, 2023: https://www.sac-isc.gc.ca/eng/1541187352297/1541187392851

any adoption with the other half of a child's family group that can offer true permanence and care. People related to the child should not be taken away from the child. I shudder to think about how many grandparents and family members who have wanted to adopt have formally been denied by McFamily. If those family members lack sufficient financial resources (if they are seniors on fixed incomes, for instance), they are unable to resist McFamily placing colonial and political considerations over the best interest of the children. The children become pawns in a politicized matter. I can only hope that our case creates new conversations and a paradigm shift away from politicizing children's well-being and future. Yet, it is our conviction that McFamily directors have not had enough judicial accountability oversight in how they have been making adoption decisions for children of mixed heritage. A shift needs to take place to consistently put the focus wholly on the best interest of the child. The result of the McFamily mandate to reduce adoption of mixed heritage indigenous children by the non-indigenous side of their families is clearly evident in longitudinal charts found in the public domain. The rate at which eligible "indigenous children" (the term is a catch-all phrase that includes mixed heritage indigenous children) are placed in adoption homes is far lower than that of their non-indigenous counterparts.[35] It's as if some of

---

[35] The data in the website charts indicate that indigenous adoption placements, which includes mixed heritage children, have been on the decline over the past four years. See: Government of British Columbia, "Adoption Services, Performance Indicators," accessed April 8, 2023: https://mcfd.gov.bc.ca/reporting/services/adoption-services/performance-indicators. Also see Representative for

these children are hostages in the system. It has been noted that "colonization...has a new name...it's evolved into the foster care system," which has become the "modern-day residential school system."[36]

Children and Youth, "B.C. Adoption & Permanency Options Updates," August 2019, accessed April 8, 2023:
https://rcybc.ca/wp-content/uploads/2019/09/rcy_adoptionupdate-final-aug2019_0.pdf. Especially see page 10: "Adoption: Number of children and youth in permanent care with adoption aftercare plans." The non-indigenous home data shows a decrease over the four years from 2016 to 2019. Emily Lazatin and Simon Little, "Children's watchdog warns adoptions lagging in B.C," Global News, December 13, 2017.

[36] Teresa Wright, "Foster care is modern-day residential school system: Inuk MP Mumilaaq Qaqqaq" (CBC News, June 4, 2021).

Chapter 10
Adoption:
A Forever Family

In his book *Tenacious Solidarity,* Walter Brueggemann includes a sobering chapter titled, "Children: Taken as Hostages."[37] He argues that we need a different worldview from the current secular, predatory, greedy, and idolatrous economic and political system that extracts, commodifies, and oppresses the vulnerable. He says: "In the big world of power, children are collateral damage who may happen to be in the way of relentless ambition. They are at best an inconvenient statistic, exceedingly vulnerable to the savage power of predatory confiscation. They are regularly dismissed as nameless...only in the counter-community that stands over against the big world of power do children register. In that counter-world they have names, identities, and futures."[38] Brueggemann offers a historical review of how children have been treated and says that "we live in a hostage-taking commodity system. And the reason the children need defense is that there is a vigorous offence against them. The commodity system cannot flourish without hostages." He says it is important to recognize that "children are

---

[37] Walter Brueggemann, "Totalized Techne vs. Neighborly Metis," *Tenacious Solidarity: Biblical Provocations on Race, Religion, Climate, and the Economy*, edited by Davis Hankins (Minneapolis, MN: Fortress Press, 2018).

[38] Ibid, 291.

[our] most precious treasure."[39] This means we should be advocates for children who are abandoned or orphaned,[40] be the solution in providing a home for these children,[41] and recognize that caring for and defending children—not leaving anyone behind—is grounded in Transcendent Character.[42] My wife and I desperately wanted our grandchild to be taken out of the government system (a place where she was just a name or known by her initials, a statistic, and an ethnic designation) and have the best possible chance of growing up with opportunities in her own family.

Patricia Irwin Johnston comments that "Adoption is intended to be a permanent placement...and make new legal ties—as well as emotional, financial, and supportive ties—to the family of adoption."[43] This means that "by law, adoptive parents become the legal, moral, and psychological parents to their children. Adoption is lifelong."[44]

In the course of the negotiations with McFamily, we found we needed to engage a lawyer to advise and assist us in the process of the adoption. This was because of the complexity of the issues that were thrust upon us. Once the adoption process was set in motion, we had to educate ourselves on how we would integrate our granddaughter into benefits, our will, and other financial matters. We needed to review all of the records of our granddaughter's history. We

---

[39] Ibid, 302.

[40] Ibid, 303.

[41] Ibid, 303.

[42] Ibid, 304.

[43] Patricia Irwin Johnston, *Adoption is a Family Affair: What Relatives and Friends Must Know* (London, UK: Jessica Kingsley Publishers, 2012), 25.

[44] Ibid, 27-28.

needed to review the adoption proposal package and finalize the adoption care plan, the cultural plan, and the openness agreement. Moving forward with adoption required us to become informed on legal matters pertaining to adoption/parental leave, Employment Insurance, and provincial employment standards (in regards to adoptive parents' rights).

We were assigned a terrific adoption social worker, who did an incredible job assisting us through the multifaceted process. Significant meetings with the adoption worker happened in the first month of 2020, and our grandchild had a McFamily interview at that time. We received the Notice of Placement at the end of 2020 and began our six-month adoption placement period. During the first month of 2021, we experienced what felt like a rite of passage. Two social workers came to the house, one with a large chalkboard that had inscribed on it "Adoption Day, [with the date written]." There were multiple papers to sign (the process felt as complex as signing the papers for the purchase of a house). Photos were taken of the various papers being signed, including a certificate of adoption signed by all three members of the family. That evening, friends came to celebrate with us. Congratulations poured in through emails and phone calls from friends, family members, and work colleagues on the adoption. The adoption order was finally completed in 2021 in Supreme Court. As strange as this may sound, on that day, our granddaughter also became *legally* our daughter. We felt we had a double role and a double blessing. We could feel the gravity of one Jewish poetic text that says, "Children are a generous heritage and legacy, one of God's best gifts."

An international adoption by strangers costs between $20,000 and $50,000. Since we were adopting a biological family member, we should not have had to pay amounts like that. However, the costs in stress, time, resources, and money to take the matter to Supreme Court were enormous. We were left with many lingering doubts about the gap between the practices of McFamily and the law (the ruling of the Supreme Court).

The question arises: Who can you write to in regards to the decision making of McFamily directors when they make decisions regarding mixed heritage children? Politicians? An ombudsman? Let me focus my answer. Our advice to families in a situation similar to ours is: don't waste your time (months and years) with McFamily. Go directly to a lawyer and apply to the courts under provisions of the Family Law Act.

Chapter 11
Saying Goodbye

In September 2021, we received a phone call telling us that our granddaughter's birth mother had passed away due to a sudden heart attack. She had had a long struggle with congenital heart disease. She had died on the evening of September 10, 2021, the date of my wife's parents' wedding anniversary. We spent the day trying to verify the news.

On Sunday, September 12, 2021—the day Canadians celebrate Grandparents Day—we had to do the hardest thing we have ever done: tell our adopted child that her birth mother, whom she had not seen for almost two years, was dead. We sat her down with her teddy bear, held her little, eight-year-old hands, and looked her in the eyes. She was smiling. Pause a moment and think of the disparity between the safe family environment she was in and the news we were having to tell her. We told her, "We have some very sad news to tell you. You will not forget this moment for the rest of your life. Your mother had a heart attack and is dead." The smile evaporated, and the child burst into tears, crying into the back of her teddy bear. The three of us sat huddled together, crying over the loss. We hugged Jaded, comforted her, and reassured her, "We are here for you."

No matter how troubled the parents are, in the eyes of a child they are always Mommy and Daddy. It is very sad that a mother, who battled with deep issues most of her short life, was never able to live life to her full potential. Some of her issues seem to be attributable to the intergenerational impacts of family systems. If there is a message to grandparents out of all of this, it is to continue to fight for your grandchildren's rights to a safe and loving home where they can be given a chance to fulfill their full potential in life and be the best version of themselves. We encourage grandparents to step up and take on the extremely challenging task of caring for these children. For sure, many grandparents don't have the courage to do it, but experience in the trenches of life equips older adults to make a difference.

In September 2021, by an almost miraculous arrangement of logistics, we were able to fly with our grandchild to the funeral of her mother in another region of the country. It was the high point of the COVID-19 pandemic. We left the airport and eventually drove onto the agricultural lands of the band our daughter-in-law was from. Leaving the highway, we turned onto a dirt road that led to an old log house, where the casket had been for three days. Members of the band had been conducting a wake for four days up to this point (viewings, prayers, and a nighttime big fire). We met members of the band and the mother of our daughter-in-law, and we hugged and wept together. It felt as if we were stepping back in time to a place where ancient practices of closure were conducted in a liturgy that was understood by all who were present. The old house stood like a lighthouse in the midst of fields of golden hay. As we entered through the front door, we found ourselves in a large room where three medicine men (two with braided hair and one with a black cowboy hat) were sitting in a circle in the middle of the floor. In front of them was a box about two feet long, eight inches wide, and four inches deep, and on top of it was a long, decorated peace pipe. There was a bowl about the size of two cupped hands containing sage, cedar, or sweet grass, and it was being used by the medicine men for smudging. Then, they passed around the peace pipe, each person taking a puff. Prayers were said by one of the men in their language at intervals throughout the ceremony. Then they would stand, and the three would play hand drums and sing native chants. In my own grief, I could feel the drumming in the center of my soul as it hit heavy on the beat and then shuffled or was accented on the offbeat. This rhythm is the first thing we become conscious of in our mother's womb, and now it echoed as a memorial for a mom who had struggled. I felt that this beat connected all of us in the room in a sacred expression. My guess is that members of her culture have been using the drum in sacred expression for thousands of years before churches gave permission to use drums in their sacred expressions.

The shape of the liturgy seemed to be like this: passing of the peace pipe and prayers (in the native language); drumming (with everyone standing up); prayers (with everyone sitting down and squatting); drumming (with everyone standing up and a line of three women criers); prayers (with everyone sitting down and squatting); drumming (with everyone standing up and a line of three women criers). This continued for two to three hours. During the drumming, various lines of three women would all stand up with the drummers and sing the native chants or cries.

Interspersed within this liturgy, various family members would share memories. Those speaking included our daughter-in-law's paternal grandfather, an elder and language teacher from the band, and our daughter-in-law's mother, Pandora. When I was invited to share, I described how we had met our daughter-in-law (recalling that she was shy and beautiful, inside and out), how we had welcomed her into our family, how we had given them a wedding and helped them find housing, and finally how we had struggled to help them and our grandchild Jaded. I thanked those present for welcoming us and giving us a place to bring our grief, which was weighing so heavily on us this week. There were many tears shed.

And then we lined up with our grandchild for a last view of the open casket where her mother was lying. I stood with her. Seeing her mom, she commented, "She looks like a doll!" I placed my hand on my daughter-in-law's head. We said goodbye, and then I shook hands with others on the way out through the door. I could hear the mother wailing, brokenhearted, inside the building as we all waited outside for the pallbearers to bring the casket out. Her loud wailing and crying weighed heavy on my heart. We traveled with the casket to the burial grounds, which were only about a kilometer away.

The six-foot-deep hole had already been dug, my daughter-in-law was lowered into the grave, and a native blanket was placed over the casket. More drumming and native prayers followed, and then I joined the men as we worked to move a back-breaking mound of dirt into this deep hole. Every shovel of dirt I threw into that hole was an expression of my deep sadness at the loss of this young life and the personal grief I felt over this. We shoveled and sweated in shifts—there was no tractor to move the dirt as there is in city cemeteries. At the north end of the grave, a giant Celtic cross was placed, with her birth date and date of passing. Each of us encircled the grave once, some placing flowers or stones on the periphery of the grave (not on top of it, as the band held a belief that this would interrupt her journey to the ancestors). The elders instructed that we were not to look back (not even in our car rear-view mirror), as this was considered holding her spirit back from leaving this place. We went back to the old log cabin in the midst of the golden hayfields to share bannock, rest on the porch, and tell stories. One of my daughter-in-law's family members told me, "When the government told us about a family wanting to adopt Jaded, we were not told that it was family wanting to adopt. We thought it was by strangers." I was shocked to think that the relatives in the band would have been misled like that by some intermediary or government representative —perhaps to manipulate the outcome and the optics. We had sent a video of ourselves to the adoption directors (Mr. Bureaucrat and Ms. Heartless) to pass on to the band. We pondered if Jaded's family in the band had seen that video. Was that video used by the directors Mr. Bureaucrat and Ms. Heartless to profile us and differentiate us from the heritage of our grandchild? It is significant that, not just Jack (the birth father), but also Jill (the birth mother) and her mother (Jaded's maternal grandmother Pandora), Jaded's primary First Nations relatives, were all outspoken in favor of my wife and me adopting Jaded. The opposition to the adoption was bent into broader issues of colonial assimilation by other intermediaries, with different agendas, who never knew the child.

My wife later told me that, when we had arrived at the reserve, our granddaughter said she saw a woman in the tall hayfields waving at her and then disappearing. She said it looked like her mother.

Chapter 12
Identity Formation:
The Long and Winding Road

Naturally speaking, adoption is one alternative means to having a family. An adopted child takes on the name of the adoptive parents, is given legal rights, and is forever after identified with that family. However, identity also includes ancestral history. Being adopted means belonging, and being adopted provides a sense of security, psychological stability, and peace for a child.

At times, our granddaughter has had other children at her school sometimes ask, "Why does your grandmother always pick you up after school and not your mother?" Thankfully, Jaded's adoption kept her in her extended family group, but there will continue to be questions around her identity and birth parents. In trying to help Jaded with her identity, my wife and I were intentional and proactive in giving her opportunities to become familiar with her blend of cultural heritages, which are First Nations and Euro-Canadian. We introduced her to family traditions, family history, traditional clothing, and foods, such as her Italian grandmother's pasta sauce. We were also intentional in introducing her to First Nations cultural contexts and foods. On many occasions, we visited First Nations museums and cultural contexts with her. We introduced her to foods such as bannock, elk stew, and wild berries. Our family is a mixed-race family.

Our intention is to leave Jaded a legacy that will provide her with a good foundation for her life. Tomorrow is never promised to us. As we enter the last quarter or third of our lives, it is our dream that we will still be there for our granddaughter when she graduates from high school and university, when she marries, and when she has her own children.

Social Darwinism offers a constructive viewpoint on grandparents and kinship adoption. Evolutionary theory identifies kinship adoption as being driven by "psychological mechanisms" in grandparents, where the "helping behavior directed [towards] genetic relatives"[45] is a form of altruistic behavior invested in the well-being and future of their grandkids.[46] Historically, traditional, cultural, and religious belief systems have connected with the idea that grandparents have a vested interest in the well-being and future of their grandkids. It is not always recognized that most world religions have a positive perspective on kinship adoption. Buddhism, for example, focuses on what is the best choice for the child.[47] In Islam, there are "guidelines [that] do allow for adoption, [with] biological relatives [being] usually first in line to provide care."[48] In Hindu belief

---

[45] "Evolutionary Theory of Kinship," *Encyclopedia.com*, accessed July 21, 2023:
https://www.encyclopedia.com/social-sciences/applied-and-social-sciences-magazines/kinship-evolutionary-theory

[46] William D. Hamilton, "The genetical evolution of social behavior, 1 and 2," *Journal of Theoretical Biology*, 7 (1964):1-52.

[47] American Adoptions, "Giving Your Child Up for Adoption in Buddhism," accessed July 4, 2021:
https://www.americanadoptions.com/pregnant/buddhist-giving-baby-up-for-adoption

[48] American Adoptions, "Giving Your Child Up for Adoption in Islam," accessed July 4, 2021:

and practice, there is no bar to grandparents adopting their grandchildren through a cultural and legal process.[49] In Sikh religious belief and practice, adoption within one's own extended family and close relatives is well understood. Given that 85% of the world's population holds some kind of traditional, cultural religious worldview,[50] it is not that hard to recognize that there is a worldwide common sense convention around the validity of grandparents adopting their own grandchildren.

Jaded has been told that her first name means "The Almighty watches over me." The name she bears is also a part of her self-identity. A variety of texts in the Jewish faith give insight into Yahweh's (God's) attitude regarding the care of children and people. Psalm 68:6 says, "He (Yahweh) sets the lonely in families." Isaiah 58:7 speaks of the needs of destitute members of one's own family and urges people "not to turn away from your own flesh and blood." Psalm 27:10 affirms, "Though my father and mother forsake me, Yahweh will receive me." Multiple texts in Proverbs (3:27-28, 11:25, 14:21, 14:31, 16:19, 31:8-9) instruct people to advocate for justice and speak up for those who cannot speak for themselves; this most

---

https://www.americanadoptions.com/pregnant/islam-can-i-give-a-child-up-for-adoption

[49] The Hindu Adoptions and Maintenance Act, 1956, accessed October 10, 2021: https://indiankanoon.org/doc/946025/?_cf_chl_jschl_tk_=pm d_6vZWyKgNTcLRt6U5Rxq3iAsZqmVRJv7pTKKSrWhi0lY-1633877657-0-gqNtZGzNAlCjcnBszQhl

[50] World Population Review, "Religion by Country 2023," accessed July 4, 2023: https://worldpopulationreview.com/country-rankings/religion-by-country

certainly includes a range of needy people, of which children are at the top of the list. Orthodox Judaism has a strong tradition of grandparents being engaged with their grandchildren's worldview formation and upbringing. Deuteronomy 4:9 says, "Teach...your children and...your children after them." Exodus 10:2 says, "Tell your children and your grandchildren...that you may know that I am the Lord." Psalm 145:4 says, "One generation commends your works to another." Other texts advocating for grandparents' engagement with grandchildren include Deuteronomy 6:1-2, Deuteronomy 32:7, Job 8:8-10, Psalm 22:30-31, Psalm 78:5-7, Psalm 102:18, Psalm 145:4, and 3 John 4. The Hebrew canon contains cases of Moses being adopted by Pharaoh's daughter (Exodus 2:10) and Esther being adopted by Mordecai (Esther 2,7,15)

In the Christian traditions (Catholic, Orthodox, and Protestant), Jesus is recognized as being adopted. There is an understanding that in the naming of Jesus in Matthew 1:21, Joseph formally adopted Jesus as his own and became his guardian and protector, which would mean officially recognizing Jesus as an heir and a son. The implications are massive because Joseph was of the line of King David, meaning that Jesus officially became recognized as a "son of David." When people become Christians, they speak of it as joining a spiritual family. Ephesians 1:4-5 says, "In love [God] predestined us for adoption to sonship [and daughtership]." The apostle Paul borrowed the term "adopted" from Hellenistic culture and Roman law and used it as a metaphor for being transferred into a faith family. In the first century, under Roman law, an adopted son or daughter was considered the same as a child born into the family. Paul drew on Roman law regarding adoption in Galatians 4:4-5, where he said,

"God sent his son...that we might receive adoption to sonship." The theological understanding is that people are caught in an oppressive status and need to be expedited out of a liminal situation in order that they might enter this new family. Theologians argue that the heart of the Good News is that a Heavenly Father adopts humans who receive him by faith (John 1:12-13). Adoption takes people out of captive conditions, changes their legal status, transforms them, and makes them heirs of innumerable benefits in the family of God.[51]

When a family adopts a child, there is a whole new lease on life. My wife and I knew a couple who were serving in an overseas organization in Taiwan and who adopted a First Nations son and a Taiwanese daughter. The adopted baby girl's mother worked in a brothel, and the father was in prison. The importance of that adoption, which rescued that girl from a possible destiny on the streets, cannot be understated. The new family meant a bright future for her. Another Chinese Canadian couple we knew were married for many years. When they realized they were infertile, they engaged with McFamily to adopt a Korean baby. What a joy when that adoption was complete! In one social context, I asked, "Are there any visitors here?" This little adopted boy raised his hand and said out loud, "Here I am." I thought, "Yes, there you are, adopted into more than you could ever dream of."

The theological analogy of adoption means that, because they are being welcomed into a healthier

---

[51] John Piper, "Adoption: The Heart of the Gospel" (MICAH Fund Adoption Enrichment Seminar, Minneapolis, February 10, 2007), accessed June 28, 2023:
https://www.desiringgod.org/messages/adoption-the-heart-of-the-gospel

family, legal adoptees are extended an inheritance and a destiny that are greater than winning the lottery. In multiple concrete, psychological, metaphorical, and spiritual ways, adoption dramatically changes the adoptee's life. Perhaps one of the most powerful things we can be a part of is a culture of adoption. Why? Because every child matters! Canada has a population of 40 million, but only about 1,200 children a year are adopted by the approximately 65% of Canadians who are adults. This, too, is something that should change. A culture of adoption is profoundly life-affirming. These chapters in the journey of our family are a reminder that adoption should never be about political battles (trying to correct historic colonial wrongs), but about the "best interest of the child," to give the child a hope and a future. The words of a now deceased college friend are instructive. He said that our attitude in difficult situations should never be, "I have to do this," but rather, "I get to do this."

The focus of this book has been on what is in the best interest of the child, the use of power by agencies such as McFamily, and the prejudice adoptive grandparents and other alternative families can suffer in the marketplace (with taking adoption leaves, for instance). I intentionally did not give a lengthy discussion on the impacts and costs to us as grandparents primarily because, as McFamily often states, this is not about the grandparents or the grandparents' feelings. In the McFamily system, impacts on the grandparents are irrelevant. The emotional, psychological, and spiritual upheaval my wife and I experienced in the midst of this journey were dismissed in the adoption process. In their deliberations, McFamily refused to recognize that we had lost our only child to mental illness, addiction, and a neurodegenerative disorder and that sending the child to live with others who were not related would essentially mean the loss of our only grandchild. This would have been the end of our family line, but McFamily didn't care about that. Those who undertake to be custodial grandparents can potentially experience significant opposition, in addition to possibly suffering "negative personal, interpersonal, and economic consequences, including poorer physical and mental health."[52] It is a road that can have many hidden costs, including "more isolation from age peers...strain [on] marriages and disruption of life plans."[53] The couple must also resolve their disappointment with an adult child who might take the situation for granted. There is the grief of having been pulled into the need to adopt a grandchild. There is the challenge of aiding the grandchild in the loss of the parents. Grandparents who adopt have "little in common with the parents of their grandchild's friends."[54] Most of this is invisible to outsiders. However, there is also a positive way of looking at accepting responsibility to care for one's grandchild. It "can enhance a grandparent's sense of purpose in life and contribute to feelings of maintaining the family's continuing identity and well-being."[55] Research has identified that adoptive grandparents benefit grandchildren behaviorally and academically because they provide a "safety net" of "love, security,

---

[52] Hayslip and Kaminski, "Grandparents Raising their Grandchildren," 262.

[53] Ibid, 262-263.

[54] Ibid, 264.

[55] Ibid, 263.

encouragement, and structure for grandchildren."[56] When circumstances make it necessary and possible, adopting one's grandchild can be in the best interest of the child. My wife and I have realized that adopting our granddaughter, a course pursued in the best interest of the child, might be our greatest legacy.

[56] Ibid, 263.

Epilogue

All human stories are dynamic and evolving. Therefore, a lesson for all of us is that we should never give up hope in seeing the changes we may be longing for in our family and social networks. At the close of Chapter 12, the picture for Jack looked grim. As a handicapped widower, his life was slipping deeply into an unhealthy lifestyle of severe grief, health challenges, and addiction. We braced ourselves for all possible outcomes—and then Jack hit bottom with a crisis event that created a hot leap of change. Since that event, there has been a significant development in Jack's narrative. In the past several years, he has made a 180-degree turn—his life is now going in the opposite direction. This is a reminder that a crisis can bring a jump forward, an unexpected change for the better. Jack pursued treatment and counseling for his unresolved grief and bereavement. He received medical reassessments for his handicaps and neurodegenerative disorder. He participated in a recovery program. And he joined a community that has helped to support him with his physical, emotional, and spiritual well-being while providing social support. Jack has moved into a home in a new community, and his relationships with us and Jaded are slowly being restored. He is on a new trajectory, and his compass setting is once again a Hopeful one.

Deo gratias

References

American Adoptions. "Giving Your Child Up for Adoption in Buddhism." Accessed July 4, 2021: https://www.americanadoptions.com/pregnant/budhist-giving-baby-up-for-adoption

American Adoptions. "Giving Your Child Up for Adoption in Islam." Accessed July 4, 2021: https://www.americanadoptions.com/pregnant/islam-can-i-give-a-child-up-for-adoption

Brueggemann, Walter. "Totalized Techne vs. Neighborly Metis," *Tenacious Solidarity: Biblical Provocations on Race, Religion, Climate, and the Economy.* Edited by Davis Hankins. Minneapolis MN: Fortress Press, 2018: 3-28.

Casper, Lynn M., and Kenneth R. Bryson. "Across the generations: Co-resident grandparents and their grandchildren." Paper presented at the Annual Meeting of the Population Association of America, Chicago, IL, 1998: 1-20.

City News. "Many Canadians are raising their grandchildren: Statistics Canada." Vancouver News 1130, April 14, 2015. Accessed April 9, 2023: https://vancouver.citynews.ca/2015/04/14/many-canadians-are-raising-their-grandchildren-statistics-canada/

"Evolutionary Theory of Kinship," *Encyclopedia.com*, accessed July 21, 2023: https://www.encyclopedia.com/social-sciences/applied-and-social-sciences-magazines/kinship-evolutionary-theory

Fuller-Thomson, Esme. *Grandparents Raising Grandchildren in Canada: A Profile of Skipped Generation Families.* Working paper No. 132. Hamilton, Ontario: SEDAP, McMaster University, 2005: 1-48.

Government of British Columbia. "Adoption Services, Performance Indicators." Accessed April 8, 2023: https://mcfd.gov.bc.ca/reporting/services/adoption -services/performance-indicators

Government of British Columbia. "Children and Youth in Care, Case Data and Trends." Accessed July 4, 2021: https://mcfd.gov.bc.ca/reporting/services/child-protection/permanency-for-children-and-youth/performance-indicators/children-in-care

Government of Canada. "Reducing the number of Indigenous children in care." Accessed April 8, 2023: https://www.sac-isc.gc.ca/eng/1541187352297/1541187392851

Hamilton, William D. "The genetical evolution of social behavior, 1 and 2," *Journal of Theoretical Biology*, 7 (1964):1-52.

Hayslip, Bert, and Patricia L. Kaminski. "Grandparents Raising their Grandchildren: A Review of the

Literature and Suggestions for Practice," *The Gerontologist,* Vol. 45, No. 2 (April 2005): 262-269.

Ipsos. "Adoption in Canada." Accessed April 9, 2023: https://www.ipsos.com/en-ca/adoption-canada#:~:text=There%20are%20currently%20more%20than,who%20were%20adopted%20in%20Canada.

"Jack Wester (Obituary)," *The Canadian Encyclopedia,* December 15, 2013. Accessed July 5, 2021: https://www.thecanadianencyclopedia.ca/en/article/jack-webster-obituary

Johnston, Patricia Irwin. *Adoption is a Family Affair: What Relatives and Friends Must Know.* London, UK: Jessica Kingsley Publishers, 2012.

Joslin, Daphne, and Anne Brouard. "The prevalence of grandmothers as primary caregivers in a poor pediatric population," *Journal of Community Health,* 5 (1995): 383-401.

Kane, Laura. "Indigenous heritage doesn't overrule other factors in adoption: B.C. Court" CTV News, August 9, 2017.

Lazatin, Emily, and Simon Little. "Children's watchdog warns adoptions lagging in B.C." Global News, December 13, 2017.

Legal Affairs and Justice. "Adoption and Indian Registration." Accessed July 5, 2021: https://www.afn.ca/wp-content/uploads/2020/01/17-19-02-06-AFN-Fact-

Sheet-Adoption-and-Indian-Registration-final-revised.pdf

Milan, Anne, and Brian Hamm. "Across the generations: Grandparents and grandchildren," *Canadian Social Trends*, Winter 2003. Statistics Canada website, Catalogue No. 11-008, 6. Accessed April 8, 2023: https://www150.statcan.gc.ca/n1/en/pub/11-008-x/2003003/article/6619-eng.pdf?st=0AOcjSku

Minkler, Meredith, and Kathleen M. Roe. *Grandmothers as caregivers: Raising children of the crack cocaine epidemic.* Newbury Park, CA: Sage Publications Inc., first edition, 1993.

McNamara, Tara. "The 15 Top Family Films About Adoption," *HuffPost*, December 6, 2017. Accessed December 13, 2019: https://www.huffpost.com/entry/the-top-15-family-films-a_b_6331544

Papp, Leslie, Tanya Talaga. and Jim Rankin. CYCNET, Feature: Nobody's Children. Accessed October 10, 2021: https://cyc-net.org/features/ft-nobody'schildren.html

Papp, Leslie, Tanya Talaga, and Jim Rankin. CYCNET, "Canada: More than 20,000 await adoption, but most remain wards of the state." Accessed April 9, 2023: https://cyc-net.org/profession/readarounds/ra-papp.html

108

Piper, John. "Adoption: The Heart of the Gospel." MICAH Fund Adoption Enrichment Seminar, Minneapolis, February 10, 2007. Accessed June 28, 2023: https://www.desiringgod.org/messages/adoption-the-heart-of-the-gospel

Representative for Children and Youth. "B.C. Adoption & Permanency Options Updates." August 2019. Accessed April 8, 2023: https://rcybc.ca/wp-content/uploads/2019/09/rcy_adoptionupdate-final-aug2019_0.pdf

Shlonsky, Aron, Barbara Needell, and Daniel Webster. "The ties that bind: A cross-sectional analysis of siblings in foster care," *Journal of Social Service Research*, 29(3), January 2003: 27-52.

Statistics Canada. "Diversity of grandparents living with their grandchildren," April 14, 2015. Accessed June 21, 2023: https://www150.statcan.gc.ca/n1/pub/75-006-x/2015001/article/14154-eng.pdf

Statistics Canada. "Grandparents living with their grandchildren, 2011" April 14, 2015. Accessed June 21, 2023: https://www150.statcan.gc.ca/n1/daily-quotidien/150414/dq150414a-eng.htm

The Hindu Adoptions and Maintenance Act, 1956. Accessed October 10, 2021: https://indiankanoon.org/doc/946025/?_cf_chl_jsc hl_tk_=pmd_6vZWyKgNTcLRt6U5Rxq3iAsZqmVRJv 7pTKKSrWhi0lY-1633877657-0-gqNtZGzNAlCjcnBszQhl

The Vanier Institute of the Family. "National Grandparents Day: New insights from Canadian Research," September 8, 2022. Accessed April 9, 2023: https://vanierinstitute.ca/national-grandparents-day-new-insights-from-canadian-research/#:~:text=Regardless%20of%20where%20they%20live,a%20happy%20National%20Grandparents'%20Day!

Wright, Teresa, "Foster care is modern-day residential school system: Inuk MP Mumilaaq Qaqqaq." CBC News, June 4, 2021.

World Population Review, "Religion by Country 2023," accessed July 4, 2023: https://worldpopulationreview.com/country-rankings/religion-by-country

Young, E. "We can do better on depictions of adoption in pop culture," *Global Comment*, May 22, 2018. Accessed December 13, 2019: http://globalcomment.com/we-can-do-better-on-depictions-of-adoption-in-pop-culture/

www.ingramcontent.com/pod-product-compliance
Lightning Source LLC
Chambersburg PA
CBHW060247030426
42335CB00014B/1621